Who Killed My Mother?
a memoir

Kory M. Shrum

This book is memoir. It reflects the author's present recollections of experiences over time. Some names and characteristics have been changed, some events have been compressed, and some dialogue has been recreated.

Although the author has made every effort to ensure that the information in this book was correct at press time, the author does not assume and hereby disclaims any liability to any party for any loss, damage, or disruption caused by errors or omissions, whether such errors or omissions result from negligence, accident, or any other cause.

No part of this book shall be reproduced or transmitted in any form or by any means without prior written permission of the publisher. Although every precaution has been taken in preparation of the book, the publisher and the author assume no responsibility for errors or omissions. Neither is any liability assumed for damages resulting from the use of information contained in this book or its misuse.

All rights reserved.

Copyright © 2021 by Kory M. Shrum

Cover design and art direction by Jasie Gale

Editing by Toby Selwyn

ISBN: 978-1-949577-52-5

*For anyone who has had to put themselves back together again.
And again.*

AN EXCLUSIVE OFFER FOR YOU

Connecting with my readers is the best part of my job as a writer. One way that I like to connect is by sending 2–3 newsletters a month with a subscribers-only giveaway, free stories, and personal updates (read: pictures of my dog).

When you first sign up for the mailing list, I send you freebies away. If exclusive stories and giveaways sound like something you're interested in, please look for the special offer in the back of this book.

Happy reading,

Kory M. Shrum

PREFACE

This is a true story. Probably the most honest story I've ever told in my life. In case you know me from any of the novels I've published as Kory M. Shrum, or from any of the poetry I've published as K.B. Marie, I wanted to make it clear upfront that what you're about to read is *not* a product of my imagination.

This happened. All of it.

That said, there are a few "lies" contained within. First and foremost, I told a couple of "lies" when it came to names. Some of the names were changed to protect people still living, or even if they were dead, their children. My uncle's name isn't Joe. My aunt isn't Renee. Shay isn't Shay. And no, my mom didn't marry three men named David—though she really did marry three men with the same first name.

However, my name, my wife's name, my friends' names, and even my dog's name are real—which I used with permission. Fair enough, it's questionable about whether the dog actually consented to having his name used. I asked, he gave me his paw, we shook. That counts, right?

And I didn't feel right changing my mother's name, so hers is accurate, too.

The other small "lie" pertains to dialogue. I did rely on actual text messages and recorded phone calls as much as possible, yet sometimes a sentence said aloud or texted just sounds stupid on the page.

So in this regard, I do admit to taking a few liberties with dialogue here and there for the sake of flow. I corrected word choice and grammar or clarified when necessary. But that's it. I never changed the meaning or intention of anything said.

Apart from these "lies", everything else, I'm afraid to say, is true.

Very, *very* true.

A moment of silence
for the long-awaited death
of an uneasy mind. And the belt I've worn
all my life, ever tight across my chest,
removed, put to bed.

But then I will pick up the phone. I'll dial
her number and find no one is waiting.

—excerpt of the poem "after everything, I'll miss her" from the collection *Then Came Love*

CHAPTER ONE

When I wake, the first thing I do is grab my cell phone, like everyone else, and see I've missed a call.

Mom New Cell, it says.

I decide to listen to the voicemail first before returning her call. It's important to prepare myself for conversations with my mother. They are, in their own way, treacherous battles fought over deep ravines. Sudden drops abound.

The voicemail will give me a clear read on what I'm walking into. A glimpse of the emotional landscape I'm being asked to traverse.

Will it be another plea for money? Or an emotional whirlwind where she tells me how stuck she feels, how trapped and scared about her future? Maybe it will be more complaints about the no-good heroin addict brother who steals her cash and sometimes beats her.

Perhaps she just needs another good cry about her mother, my grandmother, who died just four months ago.

Listening to her, being there for her in these ways, is all that I can do now.

From the flat of my back, while dappled sunlight dances across the comforter, I play the message. But it isn't my mother's voice emitting through the speakers.

The call that comes through at 8:58 on the morning of July 4th, 2020, is from her brother. In the nineteen-second message, in the slow, Tennessean drawl I've known all my life, he says:

"Kory, this is your uncle Joe. I need you to call me right now. I need you to call me *right now*. If my voice is putting fear in you, that's good. It's about your momma."

Putting fear in me—that's *good*?

What the hell is he talking about?

I sit up in bed and play the message again. With each second, my heart climbs higher, from my ribcage up into my throat, and knocks wildly against my vocal cords.

My wife, who'd been reading on her phone beside me, turns and asks, "What's wrong?"

I can't answer her. It's impossible to speak.

Now it's 9:41 a.m.

I call him back.

He doesn't answer.

"Babe, what's happening?" Kim asks again. Now she's the one sitting up. And the little pug sleeping on my feet, Charley, lifts his head, wondering if we're really getting up, or if this is a false start.

Kim places a hand on my back. "Are you okay?"

I'm shaking, and not from the chilly morning. In Michigan, mornings can be chilly even in July. No, I'm shaking because I'm afraid of what's coming. Because I *absolutely* know what's coming as my fist squeezes, relaxes, squeezes again, the phone in my hand.

I try to call Joe again at 10:01. But he doesn't answer for a second time.

"He's going to tell me she's dead." I refresh the home

screen of my cell phone over and over and over as if this will conjure an answer.

It rings at 10:06.

I skip the polite greetings. "What's going on?"

"Your momma's gone," he says.

And the world stops.

The silence in the dark bedroom of my house stretches infinite.

Finally, I whisper, "What?"

"She's gone. Your momma's gone."

Here my mind divides itself. There is the Kory in bed wrapped in covers, listening to the words poured rapid fire from her uncle's lips. Then there is the Kory who is outside of herself, watching it all, observing this moment as if from a great distance. This Kory is noting the apparent shock, the disbelief as if all of this is happening to someone else.

I manage to ask, "How?"

"I don't know. I came into her room this morning and found her dead in her bed. Her face was blue. *Dead* blue."

"Where is she now?" I ask. And immediately think, *As if she could move. What a stupid question.*

"In her room. I called the police and they're on their way."

I'm unsure if he's crying or if his voice is shaking with adrenaline. The three dogs, my mother's two mutt terriers and my uncle's chihuahua, are yapping in the background. From the sound of it, they're running circles around his feet.

My treacherous mind remembers dogs will eat a corpse. Didn't I read that somewhere?

I hope he's closed her bedroom door.

To tell you the truth, I'd expected myself to be more prepared for this moment.

For most of my life, I've lived in fear of this very

conversation. My mother had so many near misses over the years. So many moments when she absolutely should have died—but didn't.

There had been the drinking and driving, yes. But there was also the near-fatal assault. And once she was even shot.

As I grew up, a pattern formed and I began to believe that it was only a matter of time before I got *the call*. And in it, someone would tell me my mother had died in some tragic, heartbreaking way. The only thing left to do was to imagine all the possibilities.

These imaginings probably began when I was seven or eight and my mom disappeared for a few days. Her car was found in a ditch. She'd been drunk, had driven off the road, and left with the first man who'd found her. It wouldn't be the last time this happened.

Now it's finally happened. *The call*.

Yet, to my surprise, I can't believe it.

I just spoke to her yesterday. She was fine. In better spirits than she'd been in weeks.

How could she possibly be dead just hours later?

Then Joe asks, "Do you have an insurance policy on her?"

Such a bizarre question jolts me out of my wandering thoughts. "How in the world could I have an insurance policy on her?"

When my wife and I got our insurance policies, a woman with a medical kit came to our house. In our dining room, she'd drawn our blood, measured us, weighed us, had us complete detailed medical questionnaires with official-looking ink pens while we sat around the table.

They made sure we weren't secretly on death's door. From this, I assumed all policies had the same vigilant requirements.

My uncle is quick to inform me otherwise.

"Oh no," Joe assures me. "You can take up to fifty thousand out on a person without them even knowing."

My mind sticks on "without them even knowing." And $50,000 is such a specific number.

So I tell him that's not what happened when Kim and I got our policies.

"You must've gotten a big policy," he says, with more than a little interest in his voice. "How much did you get yours for?"

I don't want to tell him. Somehow in my mind, equating my life with a dollar amount seems like a dangerous game, and one I'd never want to play with *him*.

"I don't know," I say.

He laughs, a tight, bitter sound. "Yes, you do. You're lying. You sure are from this family, aren't you?"

I say nothing to this.

"Never mind," he quickly adds. "I'd hoped maybe you'd get a little something out of this, but it's fine."

He sounds angry.

"I'll take care of *everything*. I've done it for Nana, and for everybody else. Don't you worry about a damn thing."

Though he won't, in fact, take care of everything. I'll be the one that handles my mother's cremation, but that's a problem I don't yet realize I have.

I ask him again how she died.

"I don't know, I told you. I went in there and she was blue."

I can't imagine people just walking into bedrooms and finding dead people. According to the Internet, only about twenty percent of people die at home.

"Are they going to do an autopsy?" I ask, because I'm hoping someone, somewhere down the road, is going to have answers for me.

At this, he laughs. "Of course they're gonna do an autopsy. When someone as young as her dies, they're gonna check it out."

"What do you think happened?"

"She was so blue," he says again, as if this is supposed to mean something to me. "I think she took something. I don't know how, but I know what an overdose looks like, and she's blue just like that. I need to check my safe. I need to make sure everything is there."

This startles me.

Until this moment, I was under the impression my mother had died because her poor health had finally caught up to her.

Bad health had plagued my mother for years, and we're in the middle of a pandemic.

But here Joe's alluding to the possibility of an overdose. That somehow my mother got ahold of something, *took* something, and it killed her.

My mother said she'd been clean for months, on absolutely nothing at all, not even the Celexa and Seroquel prescribed for her unstable mind because Joe supposedly had taken her pills and locked them up in his safe back in March.

The safe he's referring to is his drug safe. Where he keeps his heroin and anything else he buys from the street with hopes of reselling.

My shock begins to morph into something harder. My hand fists the comforter stretching across my legs.

"You said she hadn't taken anything for a long time. You said you'd locked up even her pills. You *both* said she was completely clean."

"That's true. I did lock them up!" he insists.

"Then how could she have taken something?"

"I don't know! Maybe she broke into my safe."

My mother, five feet four and a hundred and thirty pounds, breaking into a safe like she's in *Ocean's Eleven* or something?

It doesn't help that my mother is—was—nearly blind in both eyes and had even lost her last pair of glasses months ago. I've been trying to get Joe to take her to the eye doctor, volunteering to pay for the exam and glasses, but he kept claiming the Wal-Mart Vision Center was always closed when they went.

This idea that my mother would have the patience, attention span, or even the opportunity to crack a safe is ridiculous.

"You think she *took* something?" I'm unable to hide my disbelief. I know he must hear it.

His indignation burns bright. "All I know is I went in there and found her and she's blue! The color of her face is *dead blue*."

He must mistake my silence for resignation and moves to end the call.

He lowers his voice. "Look. I know I'm never going to hear from you after this. I know you don't like me much."

He pauses, probably expecting me to do the obligatory "No, no, don't say that. I don't hate you."

I say nothing.

He adds, "I know you haven't forgiven me for what happened all those years ago. So, *so* long ago."

He's right.

Though I'm not sure it's so much a matter of forgiveness as trust.

I don't trust him.

Even as a child, even before he gave me a real reason to keep one eye open, to never turn my back, he'd felt dangerous.

And I have the good sense—most of the time—to stay away from what's dangerous.

So he's right. When this call ends, I'll have no reason to speak to him ever again.

I've only tolerated him this long because he was the official caregiver of my mother. Because speaking to her often meant going through him. Because he guarded the phone jealously, always waiting for someone to call him, probably about drugs and so his voice was the first I'd often hear.

"Your mother didn't love anyone," he tells me. "But she loved you. If heaven is what you want it to be, she's with you now."

Faced with the fact I never plan to speak to him again, I do what I think is best.

"I forgive you," I choke out. "I forgive you for everything."

Here the tears spill over at last.

What an idiot I was, to believe forgiveness would be so easy.

It'll be four hours before I receive the second, more illuminating phone call.

In the meantime, I have my cry in the bed, my wife rubbing my back, pouring apologies into my ears.

The usual "I'm so sorry" and "It's going to be okay".

Then I get up, let the dog out, and begin the normal Saturday morning clean. I don't make it very far.

In my office closet, I find a large folder of photographs that my mom sent me years ago.

I comb through them, laying them out in rows on my wooden floor as a hoard of finches sing their hearts out through the open window.

My grandmother dead. My grandfather dead. My aunt dead. My mom dead.

Joe is the only one left.

I had a feeling this was how it'd play out, he'd once said. *That I'd outlive them all.*

As I stare at each glossy face, my mind keeps reviewing the last months of my mother's life. I run the list of possible causes for her death, still believing that it must've been her body that killed her.

There are many suspects in this scenario.

There was her hepatitis C, which she'd had for almost thirty years.

Back in the nineties she'd reconnected with her first husband, a "bad guy."

Fun fact: my mother married three times in her life, and all three men shared the same first name.

When David #1 resurfaced, he introduced my mother to cocaine. But not the stylish kind that starlets snort in a bathroom at Hollywood parties before retouching their eyeliner. No, this cocaine was shot into the veins. And sharing dirty needles with the ex-husband you ran away with and married at sixteen isn't *typically* a good idea.

Fortunately, the ex nor the needles stuck around, but the hepatitis C she'd contracted did.

Living with hep C had made her tired and nauseated often. It also made her need to quit drinking imperative.

And she did quit drinking. I was proud of her for that.

If it wasn't hep C or its complications that ended her life, there was still COVID-19 to consider. By the time Joe calls me to say he's found her corpse, we're almost four months into the pandemic. The country has shut down. Everyone is scrambling to understand what the virus is and what it can do. The number of cases in Nashville is high. While it's true that my mom never leaves the house, Joe certainly does. License or not, drugs don't buy or sell themselves. Who knows what he brought home.

As a longtime smoker with poor health, my mom would've been easy pickings for a respiratory virus. She already had a hacking cough on the best of days, often pulling away from the phone, squeezing out a "Just a minute, baby" until she could catch her breath.

She'd been smoking since she was fourteen—reminding me as often as she could—that she'd quit only for the months that she'd been pregnant with me.

"When the nurse asked me if I wanted to breastfeed, I said, 'Hell no! Give me a cigarette!' I couldn't wait a minute longer. But look at you! You're *perfect*," she'd always add, beaming every time she told this story. Clearly, she believed her months of sacrifice had paid off.

Could COVID-19 leave a corpse blue in the face?

If not hepatitis C, COVID-19, or some other respiratory disease, there's still her most recent symptom to consider.

Her memory loss.

It began in March. I'd called to check in, and during the course of our conversation, she'd casually said, "So you know Nana passed."

I *hadn't* known that her mother, my grandmother, had died.

In fact, I'd called on March 3rd to check on the family and see if they'd fared all right against the tornado that had blown through Nashville the night before. My uncle, who always answered the phone, had said, "We're all right here," and hung up on me.

I thought this was rude, but not necessarily nefarious.

My mother sometimes slept the day away. If she was asleep, he wouldn't bother calling her to the phone. There was also the possibility that he was simply too high to care, knowing now that it was only his niece, and not someone looking to make a deal.

But they were *not*, in fact, "all right." My grandmother had been dead for two days and my mother had been in the hospital for nearly ten.

"No one told you?" my mother said, as if there were legions of family members that could've stepped up and informed me of the situation, and not, in fact, one compulsive liar.

"No. He didn't tell me."

It had been the Internet that had told me Nana's memorial had been on March 1st.

My mother's outrage on my behalf was touching. Until the next time I called.

"So you know Nana died," she said again.

"Yeah, you told me."

"Oh." Here she paused. Her dogs were yapping up a storm. "Did I?"

"Don't you remember?"

"I've been having problems remembering things," she said in a wistful voice.

"What do you mean you're having problems remembering things? What kind of things?"

"I was in the hospital and now I don't remember things."

This was the first time I heard about the hospital.

At this point, I asked to speak to Joe, but she didn't hand the phone over.

I refused to let this go. "Why were you in the hospital? What the hell happened?"

My mother asked Joe, and I could hear him through the phone as he said, "You had a nervous breakdown."

"I had a nervous breakdown," she parroted.

"What kind of breakdown? What caused it?"

"I don't know," she said.

"What did the doctors say? What did they treat you for?"

Finally Joe got on the phone.

My interrogations got me nowhere. Joe didn't clarify what landed my mother in the hospital, but instead spent five minutes assuring me that *they*—presumably the doctors—wanted to institutionalize her, but *he*—good brother that he was—saved her from that dark fate.

"They were lockin' everything down for the virus," he said. "I got her out of there fast. I wasn't gonna let them take *my* sister."

He took a drag on his cigarette.

I asked, "What caused her breakdown?"

"She took her pills wrong and went in."

Went in, I assumed, to the hospital.

"But they wanted to institutionalize her, and I said, '*Hell no*,' and I got her out of there."

"What about the pills?"

"I've locked them up. They're in my safe—she can't get in there."

Then why the memory loss, I wondered.

Was it some reaction to being taken cold turkey off her medication?

My mother had needed medication for decades. She was diagnosed as manic depressive when I was a kid. Later, the industry would start calling it bipolar disorder. Then, in her late forties, they'd added schizoid affective disorder onto her diagnosis because sometimes she suffered from delusions and lost touch with reality. This was especially pronounced when she'd stop sleeping.

For all of this, she was given prescriptions for Celexa and Seroquel, but her medications were tricky.

She'd had bad reactions before. In these reactions, her psychosis would be so pronounced, often terrifying. She would wander off. Forget where she was or how to get home. She'd leave a cigarette burning on a sofa arm, or a faucet running until the sink overflowed, the floors flooded. Or she'd become inconsolably angry when you asked her simple questions, or tried to stop her doing something unsafe—like driving a car.

This was back when she was still an alcoholic. Alcohol and medication don't mix. But she hadn't had an episode like this since she'd quit drinking.

What had happened this time?

"She's much better off of them," Joe told me. "Much more steady."

"What about the memory loss?"

"She's getting better every day. Her mind just needs time to adjust being off 'em," he said, taking another long draw of his cigarette.

"Are you sure that's safe?"

"It's a lot safer than the alternative."

I considered this. I wasn't a doctor, and I also wasn't there in the house with them. On no front was I qualified to know what care she needed.

But the memory loss concerned me. Given her history of a traumatic brain injury, I was worried the memory loss pointed to a more serious brain issue, especially when Joe told me about the seizure.

According to him, they were standing in the kitchen when it happened. My mother had been at the counter, making herself a sandwich. They'd been talking, and suddenly, my mother's eyes had rolled up into her head and she'd dropped.

Those were his words: "She dropped."

During the seizure, she turned blue. He did compressions, trying to get her to breathe, and was successful in resuscitating her.

"Is that true?" I asked her, because there was something in Joe's telling of it that rang false for me. A lie embedded that I couldn't quite tease out.

"I don't remember," was her reply.

My mother had seizures when she was a child, the first of them when she was around eleven. This was supposedly where her mental health problems began, resulting in a suicide attempt at twelve. But as an adult, her seizures all but disappeared. Why would they come back now—*if* they'd come back?

Were the memory loss and seizure a sign that she had a lesion or something? A clot ready to break off and stop her heart?

"Why didn't you take her to the hospital?" I asked Joe. "You could've called an ambulance or something." I assumed prematurely that maybe it was impossible to carry a convulsing person. I've personally never tried.

"If it happens again, I will," he said. "I absolutely will."

All of these threads that I'm clinging to—that it could be her health that killed her, that my uncle simply didn't want to take my mother to a hospital during a deadly pandemic, that his fears were natural rather than malicious —dissolve when my phone rings at 2:25 that afternoon.

It's been four hours now of me not cleaning my house. Me lying on the sofa with my pug, Charley, snoring on my chest, when the Nashville area number flashes on my phone.

"Hello?"

"Is this Kory?" a man asks. "Leitha's daughter?"

Somewhere in the background someone speaks. The man says, "Yeah, I'm talking to her daughter now."

My heart takes off like a rabbit who's heard a twig snap. "Yes. This is she."

I sit up on the sofa, and Charley slides off of me, much to his dismay.

"I'm Detective Barnes with the Nashville Police Department. What can you tell me about your mom and her history with her brother."

"Oh…" My mind is dilating again. Making room for more impossibilities. "Oh, uh…"

A detective. A detective is calling me.

"Violent," I spit out, as if this one word answers his question. "He's assaulted her several times."

My breath is shaking but I'm quickly collecting myself.

"He struck her with a glass ashtray in 2006. It caved in her head and she had emergency surgery to let the blood out. She almost died."

I'm trying not to relive that day, but the memory swells like a wave and overtakes me.

Already I'm walking into the dark hospital room to find my mother, small and wrapped like a doll, in the bed. The layers of gauze make her head look swollen, enlarged like a bizarre, giant thumb. From her left side, a tube runs out, draining the blood that would otherwise drown her brain.

Kill her.

In the days that followed, she could smile at me but not say my name. She couldn't walk without help. She had to relearn how to speak, how to move her body.

And I had to watch.

Me sitting in her rehabilitation room. Her asking me to shave the other half of her head so her hair, always so beautiful, would grow back evenly.

Me with a razor, doing a terrible job of it, because I'm trying to be careful of the sixty-plus staples holding the left side of her scalp together. That angry, accusing hook shape of black teeth daring me to make a mistake.

That's been my role in this life, it seems.

To bear witness to her suffering, and yet have no power to stop it.

I shove the memories down, but I can't escape the familiar feelings of helplessness. Fear.

I wrestle with the old desperate need to save her.

Protect her. My mother.

The detective is still talking, his drawl deeper than my uncle's. "The condition in which her body was found, the state of her room, her clothes. And he keeps changing his story."

The condition of her body.

The state of her room.

Her clothes—

I'm certain the detective is telling me my mother has been beaten to death. That Joe lied—like he's lied so many times before—about how he found her.

That her final moments must have been full of pain, and terror. That the ashtray had come down again, but this time there was no one to make the call, to alert the police, to get her to the hospital in time.

I feel like someone has kicked me in the guts. I'm groping for air, for words. For two coherent thoughts I can string together.

"What do you mean? A-about her body?" I ask.

"She was on the bedroom floor. The room looked like it'd been tore up. Her clothes were askew. He said they had a fight about money."

Her room torn up. A fight about money.

A fight about money?

Was he telling me my mother was beaten to death by her brother over *money*?

My fear transforms into rage.

"The only money in that house was hers!" I tell him. "He didn't even have a job. *He* stole money to buy his stupid drugs. How could she steal her own money?"

The detective has no answer for this.

I'm shaking now with the effort to collect myself.

Then I ask, "You think he hurt her?"

"His story keeps changing. First, he said he found her in the bedroom. Then we started asking questions, and he said he came home and found her on the floor and *put* her in the bedroom. He says he thinks she got into his heroin and took that."

"My mother has never done heroin in her life," I grind out. "That was *his* drug."

She had vices. Absolutely. But my mother detested heroin.

The detective sighs. "To be honest with you, I think he did something to her. I just don't know that I can prove it."

I feel sick. I'm hoping I can get through the call before throwing up.

"There's still the outstanding warrant on him for the strangulation," the detective tells me. "We're going to book him for that. We're taking him in now. I'll call you once we get the autopsy results and let you know what we find."

The strangulation.

I'd forgotten about that.

When my mother called me from the bathroom and, whispering into the phone, said he'd strangled her, I'd called the police. I told them to go out there to the house and check on her.

They'd noted the bruising. Had opened the warrant.

But my uncle is very good at disappearing before the police show up. He's pulled that magic trick more times than I can count.

So they hadn't taken him in February. Or any time since.

Later, I would be on the phone with AT&T for over an hour, trying to find the exact time I'd called to report the strangulation. Turns out it had been 2:47 p.m., Saturday February 16th, 2019.

February 2019.

Just seventeen months before she died.

"Once we do the preliminary examination," the detective goes on, "I'll give you a call."

"You'll call me after the autopsy," I repeat.

"Yes, ma'am," the detective says. "Should be tomorrow or Sunday."

The call ends, and as I sit on the couch, holding my phone in the heartbeats that follow, I cross some surreal line between reality and fiction.

This can't be happening.

I didn't just get a call from a detective. He didn't just tell me my mother might have been murdered by my uncle. I'm not waiting on the results of an autopsy.

I *write* crime fiction. I don't live in it. I research, plan, and unfold investigations to entertain people. Murderers are supposed to be faceless mafiosi or perverts who bury their victims in the deep, dark woods.

He's not supposed to be my own flesh and blood.

He's not supposed to be a man my mother trusted. Relied on.

"This can't be happening," I say to no one. "It can't be."

After the nighttime calling,
the lying, the using,
the disappearing, the drinking—
if I can love her as I do
then I can love anyone. Anything.
Maybe even myself.

—excerpt of the poem "My mother, my guru" from the collection *Then Came Love*

CHAPTER TWO

When the call with the detective ends, I'm not okay. The tears that follow make my good cry in bed this morning seem like a mild malaise. Those were stoic tears.

Yet by some miracle, I manage to hold in the worst of it until Kim leaves, agreeing to do the weekend grocery trip that I've been, understandably, excused from.

She probably wants a break from all this crying. I can't blame her.

The moment she closes the front door, I collapse. Sobs wrack my body until I can't breathe.

My knees hit the rug in our living room. Apologies pour from my mouth until I'm wheezing, choking on my own snot and spit.

I cry for my mother, sure.

I can't imagine a death like the one the evidence alludes to.

Such a death brings up all my old codependent feelings of helplessness, reminding me again how many times I've tried to get her out of bad situation after bad situation and how I always, *always* failed.

The words I cry aloud on the floor of my living room, my arms wrapped around me, rocking myself back and forth into oblivion, don't emerge from fear or even grief.

I'm drowning in guilt.

"I'm sorry. I'm so sorry I chose myself over you. *I'm so sorry.* Momma, I'm sorry. *I'm sorry.*"

Because I did choose myself.

After my mother's ex calls me to say she's found my mother unconscious, after she describes the goose egg on her head and relays my grandmother's weak "Oh, her and Joe just got into it again" excuses, after the emergency surgery, after the weeks of coming straight from my classes to the rehab center where my mother was staying, after shaving her head in the handicap bathroom with a disposable razor, after all of it—I chose myself.

As she was healing, after she relearned how to talk but wasn't yet walking well, she'd agreed to come live with me.

It wasn't ideal for me, but I was ready to do anything to keep her away from Joe.

I was a busy college student, taking courses even in the summer so I could graduate with my bachelor's degree in December—because I was already a semester behind. I'd spent money and time I didn't have fixing up the spare room of my little two-bedroom duplex for her so she'd feel comfortable and welcome.

I'd bought a bed, bedding. I'd fallen off a chair and bruised the hell out of my knee trying to hang curtains for her.

A couple of weeks before she was scheduled to be released from the rehabilitation center, I received a call saying she'd left early against their wishes. Someone had signed her out. It took me a minute to find out which traitorous friend it had been, and that they'd dropped her off back at my grandmother's.

Where my uncle, the man who'd almost killed her, still lived.

I was afraid of her spending a minute more in that house with him, so I drove the hour between my university town and my grandmother's house in Nashville.

I had one condition for this arrangement. My mom could live with me as long as she liked, expense free in her own bedroom, and I'd cover us with the income I made from my two jobs: a campus job and another at the call center where I answered tech support calls for people with glitchy cell phones.

The money wasn't much. It'd be tight, but I was determined to make it work if it meant keeping all the bones in her skull intact. The rest of them, anyway.

I had only one condition.

All she had to do was not drink.

She could smoke her customary two packs a day, even though I hated it.

But *not drink*.

She'd been a drinker since I was a kid, and had more than a handful of DUIs to her name.

I was told the alcohol dependency cleared her system during her hospital stay following the ashtray incident. Considering this and the fact her drinking had already cost me so much of my peace and sanity, I didn't think this one condition was too much to ask.

I'd been wrong.

When I arrived at my grandmother's, I refused to go in because Joe was there. I told my mom to come out and meet me in the driveway, where I waited in my idling car.

My personal issue with my uncle, if we overlook how many times he's put his hands on my mother, is that he tried to wrap his hands around my throat at my grandfather's funeral in 2001 while he was high on crack cocaine.

I wasn't interested in a repeat performance and had stayed out of arm's reach since.

By the time my mom brought her things out to the car, she was pissed that I hadn't come in to help her.

A bit spitefully, I told her that if she was well enough to sneak out of the rehab center, she was well enough to carry her trash bag full of clothes to the car.

Minutes later, we stopped at the gas station, the stinging, pungent smell of gasoline seeping from the pumps. I needed gas. She asked for money to buy cigarettes. I handed it over without complaint.

Only she didn't come out with cigarettes.

She came out with a case of beer.

What followed was one of the few times I'd ever really *screamed* at my mother.

But there she was in my passenger seat with a six-pack in her lap, that she'd bought with *my* money, while all those staples in her hook-shaped scar stared back at me.

It was made worse by the fact that she seemed completely unable to understand why *I* was so upset to see her twisting the cap off a beer.

The words were out of my mouth before I could stop them. "I can't do this with you!"

"Don't be so dramatic. It's just a beer." She threw her head back and took a deep drink, the acrid smell of it blooming in the car around us.

"It's not just a beer. Look at your head. Look at your *fucking* head."

Of course, now I hated myself for yelling at her. For losing my temper while she sat there, looking so fragile and broken.

In that moment, it was clear to me that only one of us had had enough.

That nothing I did for her or offered her would pull her out of this world.

I had a choice.

I could either stay in this with her, give up on all my dreams, and go all in with my crusade to save her.

Or I could bow out.

Reinvest my energy into building the life I'd dreamed of and prayed for since I was a kid.

But I couldn't do both. My terrible grades and poor mental health told me as much. I was trying my damnedest to walk both paths at once.

And I was failing completely.

This was the moment, perhaps the first in my life, when I chose me.

I chose to believe that I could have better. Do better. I chose to believe I'd tried everything I could to help my mom, but nothing had worked. My love alone, my willingness to destroy my spirit, my heart, and my mind on the rocks of her self-destruction, wasn't enough.

It would never be enough.

So I drove my mom back to my grandmother's and stopped at the end of the driveway.

I told her to get out.

And now, fifteen years later, I've built that life I'd dreamed of. A quiet home. A loving home. No one puts their hands on each other. No one disappears in the middle of the night. I've never had a cop show up on my doorstep.

I have a caring, affectionate partner who hardly drinks so much as a glass of wine at New Year's. I have friends who care about me, who want good things for me, who worry about me.

I'm surrounded by people I trust, people who would

never hurt me intentionally. I have people I can call if I ever get into trouble—though I'm too prideful and embarrassed to ever do it.

I've completed graduate school twice. Taught writing to thousands of students. I've launched my own independent publishing company, Timberlane Press, and have published over twenty books.

I'm finally a full-time author like I always wanted to be.

I spend my days how I like, with a sweet dog close by. Breaks for tea and long walks through the neighborhood. On most nights, I sleep easy. Not all of them—but most.

It was a hard road getting here.

If I'm being honest, some days the sky presses down on me. The wind changes. Storms dark and menacing loom on the horizon. In those moments, I forget how far I've come. In those moments, I have to choose myself and this life, this happiness, all over again.

But I do it. Every time.

I choose me.

And despite all I've done, my mother is dead.

I still couldn't save her.

AT THREE A.M. I WAKE, FITFUL, FEELING SICK. THE GUILT hasn't abated. Cold sweat coats the back of my neck. I try to shake this fugue of nightmares, wishing they would dissolve like mist in the morning sunlight.

I have that drop-kicked feeling one gets when they wake to a terrible reality slowly remembered.

I run a hand down my face, trying to decide if I want to fight for more sleep or surrender to the insomnia.

The bedroom curtain sits twisted on its rod, revealing part of the window normally hidden from view. Through it, the full moon watches my silent debate.

My mom is never going to look at this moon again.

Has she ever?

Surely. In the course of her fifty-six years on this planet, she must've stared up at the night sky, likely with a cigarette burning down between her fingers, contemplating its bright, mysterious face.

Maybe on a night when she was pregnant, me sleeping inside her, she stared at this same moon and wondered where we'd be in ten, twenty, thirty years.

Could she have imagined an ending like this for herself?

There's no way I can sleep with thoughts like these.

I untangle my legs from the pug snoring on them and slip from the bed, trying not to wake Kim.

Downstairs, in my office, I turn on the lamp. Soft light filters through the paper lantern shade.

I pull my thesis off the shelf and reread the story I wrote about the ashtray incident.

Skimming the first page, I realize the ashtray incident also happened over a fourth of July weekend. What is it with Joe and the fourth of July?

If at first you don't succeed, try, try again.

I slam the thesis shut. I shuffle through the poems I wrote about her just two days before. One ominously titled: "after everything, I'll miss her"

A strange premonition.

As the poem says, *if I dial her number, no one will be waiting*.

My mother is gone.

What is left of her but our memories, our stories, the threads that bind us? All that bound her to a past she couldn't escape.

I pace my office. I feel cut through. The severance

between my mother and me is so clean, I can still feel my phantom limb.

It's taken only one day—less than a day—for me to discover a terrible, overlooked truth.

When someone you love dies—especially if your relationship wasn't ideal—there is a second death you must accept.

The death of the person.

And the death of all the hopes you had for them.

I thought I'd made peace with my mother years ago, accepted our flawed relationship and its limitations for what they were.

I can see now, as an invisible fist inside me opens and closes, grasping for what's no longer there, that I've been lying to myself.

Until this very moment, I was still holding on to *us*, to the dream that one day we could make it better. We could have something *good*.

How will I ever accept this? I've been trying to let go for over twenty years—why is it still so hard?

How will I make my peace with this?

The same way I make peace with everything, I think, and pull a yellow legal pad from my desk drawer and fish a black ink pen from a case.

For a long time I only look at the empty lines, the pen twisting between my fingers.

I catch sight of the moon again, watching through my softly lit window.

I write:

A mother like mine isn't born. Nor does she wash onto the shore like some golden-haired Aphrodite from the sea foam. A woman like her is crafted slowly, by cruel, unloving hands. To understand my mother, you have to understand the ones who made her.

My hand hovers above the paper. It trembles.

These short lines are enough to stir memories long abandoned. Twisted, misshapen things rolling beneath the surface.

"I don't know if I can do this," I tell the moon.

This—writing my way through—is what I've always done.

I know no other way.

But it's one thing to show my pain in fiction, to trace old scars as if they belong to another body, another mind. On such a stage, it's all magic tricks and good fun.

On such a stage, we both know that at the end, everything will be all right. We'll both go home and sleep soundly believing there is beauty, reason, and justice in the world.

The good people will always win. The bad people will always be punished.

But this story is different.

To tell this story will be like undressing in front of a stranger.

"Can I do it?" I ask the empty office.

The ghosts of my past—my mother's past—crowd my table.

They're waiting for an answer.

In this garden called life…
for a long time dirt is only dirt.

If I stare long enough, I can't be sure
if there was a hole at all. And how many

seeds are under there now, waking
or withering in the darkness?

—excerpt of the poem "a waste of a life" from the
   collection *Then Came Love*

CHAPTER THREE

I achieve absolutely nothing the day after my mother dies. It's a day spent on the sofa, MacBook open on my lap as I search the Internet for answers it probably doesn't have. When my eyes begin to feel like they're bleeding, my contacts fogging up and threatening to pop right out of my sockets, I take a break, but only from looking at the screen. Not from obsessing.

It's all I can talk about with my friend Katie.

"They arrested him," I say, referring to my uncle Joe.

"For her murder?" she asks.

"No, for the outstanding strangulation warrant. I don't think you can be officially charged with murder until they have conclusive evidence. They don't have that yet."

Detective Barnes summed it up well: "I think he did something to her, I just don't know that I can prove it."

My mind wrestles with the two versions of my uncle's story as I try to decide which might be more true. Katie helps me tease it apart.

"Assuming he's not lying about finding her on the floor, why didn't he call anyone when he found her?" I ask.

"Because he's a bastard," is Katie's reply.

"It's not like he doesn't know what can happen."

If my uncle can walk into my mother's room and after one look claim it was an overdose, as he did on the day of her death, then he certainly knows what an overdose *in progress* looks like. If she did take something and he found her collapsed, wouldn't he have known right away that she was overdosing?

I think so.

My aunt Renee, my mother and Joe's older sister, died of an overdose in December of 2003. Joe claims that he was with her when it happened, that he was the one desperately trying to put clothes on her before the police came, after finding her naked on her bathroom floor. Whether or not this is true, I can't say.

And what is it with my uncle walking into rooms and finding dead people? Coincidence? Or a suspicious pattern?

Either way, my uncle has been an addict for a long time. He's used crack cocaine, heroin, and all manner of pills for at least twenty years. He has said himself that he knows what an overdose looks like, and I suspect that he *does* know. Not just what a body looks like after death, but also because he would've been on the alert for those symptoms in himself.

He would've also known antidotes like naloxone exist, that overdoses can be reversed if someone gets treatment in time.

Joe had all of this knowledge when he found my mother unconscious. If he really came home and found my mother collapsed on the floor, he would've recognized it for the overdose that it was. He would've known—and yet he chose not to help her.

Why?

Of course, here, being the over-rationalizer that I am, I assume there must be a good reason. "Maybe he was too stoned to drive—"

"No." Katie stops me. She isn't having this. "He just drove home."

"Okay—he can drive but doesn't want to."

"There's a thing called an ambulance," she says.

"Right. But he didn't call for one, so maybe the phone—"

She interrupts me again. "The phone is working. You spoke to your mom the day before. And again when he called you to tell you she was dead."

"Maybe he was just scared to call the police? He doesn't have a great record with them, and there was the warrant."

"He had no problem calling them to say she was dead," she finishes. "He did that even before he spoke to you."

She's right on all counts.

The phone was working. The car was working. He was able-bodied enough to move her to the bedroom and brave enough to call the police to report her dead but not to get her the medical attention she needed? Even though he would've known exactly what was happening? What the dangers were?

I sit up on the sofa and rub my aching head. Kim reminds me to drink water. Charley carries on snoring.

"I just don't understand—" I say. Because clearly I'm still looking for a reason for this not to be true. *He didn't kill her. Please God, he didn't kill her.*

"There's nothing to understand," Katie says patiently. "He's obviously sick."

There's also the last piece of his story to reconsider.

"Do you really think my mom could've broken into his safe? She'd never do heroin in a million years, but if she could get ahold of a pill or something—"

"Okay," she says. "Let's assume he's telling the truth about locking everything in the safe. I'm sure his paranoid ass did. Are we to believe that the safe worked for all those months since your grandma died—"

"Four months," I interject.

"Yes, it worked for four months, and then, what? It just stopped working? The safe is faulty now?"

It doesn't make sense. If the story is that all the drugs in the house—even my mother's prescriptions—were locked up in the safe, how did she get ahold of something that could kill her?

It makes much more sense that any drug she came into contact with would've been a drug that he'd given her.

If he'd given it to her, he would've been the one to buy it, to know what it was. This leads me back to wondering why—*how*—he could watch her overdose without helping her.

How cold, how cruel does one have to be for that?

Of course, the only living person there that night, the only person who knows the truth of what happened, is my uncle.

But he's a liar.

How does one find the truth when the only witness is a master of deceit?

I need something concrete. Something I can understand. I need the autopsy.

The weekend passes in a haze. I'm conscious of moving from room to room, but not really clear on what I'm doing.

I'm on the sofa. I'm at the sink. I'm at the dining room table.

My wife says something.

Now the dog is looking at me expectantly, his cinnamon bun of a tail wagging hopefully.

I barely note any of this. My mind is consumed with the autopsy. What it might say. When the detective might call. What—if anything—I'm going to do with the results.

There are three parts to my mother's autopsy: an external examination of the body, an internal examination of the body, and the toxicology report.

The external examination, as the name suggests, is a review of the exterior of the body. If he beat her to death. If he wrapped his hands around her throat, or stabbed her, anything violent, the cause of death could be determined with the external examination alone.

The internal examination covers the organs like the heart, lungs, everything else, anything that happened under the skin.

If her hepatitis C caught up with her at last, if it was cirrhosis or liver disease, or lung disease from her chronic smoking. Maybe even a stroke or heart attack, blood clot in the brain…Any of that could be determined from the internal examination.

This part of the autopsy also checks for non-pathological causes.

"I want the medical examiner to look for air bubbles," the detective tells me. "In case he shot her up with an empty syringe."

I imagine my uncle chasing my terrified mother through the house with an empty syringe. I imagine her trying to shove her bedroom door closed before he busts through.

How long would it have been between the moment of injection and when the air reached her heart? How long would she have known what was coming? Unable to stop it?

Would she have tried to call me? Maybe collapsing before she could fully type my number?

Christ.

I have to stop doing this to myself.

My wild mind, though often useful, is a horrible creature when turned against myself.

Letting possible scenarios spin unchecked is wrecking me.

Stop. Please, just stop. Don't do this now.

I'll have the results for the external and internal examinations by the end of the day Monday.

I'll know more then.

In the meantime, I just have to control what I think about. I just have to get through the weekend.

Simple, right?

But my mind isn't ready to give up so easily.

You might not know anything by Monday. You might not have answers for a very long time—if ever.

It's not wrong.

If heroin really is the cause of death, it will only show on the toxicology report, the third part of the autopsy. Unlike the external and internal examinations of the autopsy, the toxicology report can take months to come back.

I have to prepare myself for that.

If the report *does* show heroin as the cause of death, I'll know he killed her. He used it to make her death look like an overdose. My mother had never—and would never, memory loss or not—do heroin.

It's telling that while he brought up the possibility of an

overdose, he never once mentioned to me that the suspected drug was heroin.

Who knows my mother's addictions better than I do? I received an intensive education for more than thirty years.

My uncle couldn't have fooled me, but he could tell the police anything.

He was counting on the system's apathy toward addicts as a mask for the perfect crime.

I suppose there's the possibility that my mother was secretly a heroin addict.

But my mother told me she was clean, and I believe her. I even have her last statement on the subject in writing.

I OPEN THE LAST LETTER I EVER RECEIVED FROM MY mother and read it again. She sent it just eleven days before she died. It's postmarked June 23rd, 2020. The address printed on the front is in my own handwriting, and the stamp is familiar. I'd known when I wrote her that if I hadn't included a self-addressed stamped envelope, I'd never hear back.

I'd sent five. She only returned one.

I know it's weird that anyone would send snail mail in the world of texting, cell phones, and the Internet, but sometimes there's no other way.

You may be shocked to know that my mother never had a smartphone. She did have my old laptop for a while, but when she spilt diet soda on it, it broke. I'd yet to cycle through another one that I could pass on to her. Buying one for herself was out of the question. Her budget simply wouldn't allow such luxuries.

Before my grandmother's death, their income consisted of my grandmother's $1,200 social security check and my mother's $795 disability check. With those two monthly checks they could pay the mortgage and utilities. Buy a bit of groceries and the supplies they needed to handroll their cigarettes. Rolling papers. Tobacco.

They couldn't afford anything else.

This is one of the reasons my mother hated Joe's heroin addiction so much. It was already difficult supporting the three of them on these two checks. It was harder when Joe would steal their money to buy his drugs. Then they wouldn't have enough to cover their bills.

Not having enough money exacerbated my mom's anxiety.

This dire financial situation got worse when my grandmother died on March 1st and the $1,200 check stopped coming. The mortgage payments were abandoned immediately. Then the utilities. I'd paid my mom's water bill sometime this past spring but couldn't cover the overdue cable bill, which had somehow ballooned to over five hundred dollars after months of going unpaid.

Then their cell phone was cut off—severing my one way of getting ahold of her.

When I called the number and found it disconnected, I was terrified.

I'd already been worried about Joe and her alone in that house without my grandmother as a buffer. With my grandmother gone, I feared it was only a matter of time before something terrible happened.

Without a way to call her, I did the only thing I could think to do.

At my dining room table, I wrote her a letter and included the five self-addressed stamped envelopes.

I begged her to write me back and tell me she was okay. In order to keep my panic from showing, I added several mundane details. I told her about the picture I was painting and updated her on the status of my vegetable garden.

When a letter finally came with my handwritten scrawl on the envelope, I tore it open with great relief. I recognized her handwriting immediately. It hadn't changed a bit.

She was alive.

After telling me that she loved me, that it was good to hear from me, she outlined the situation at the house.

She was stressed about money and didn't know how she was going to make ends meet. And for her, Joe was the cause of that stress.

In her letter she wrote, *I'm just praying Joe gets off his ass and gets a damn job quick. If he doesn't get his shit together, I don't know what I'm going to do. I'm so stressed out, I feel like I can hardly breathe. Pray for me, honey. I need it really, really badly. I need God to work a miracle in my life. I don't drink or do anything anymore, and I need Joe to do the same.*

My mom understood that she couldn't pay their bills with her disability check, let alone feed his addiction too. Nor, given the condition of her mind and health, could she work. The easiest solution for their problems would be for Joe to get a job.

From the letter, it sounded like Joe hadn't found one as of June 23rd.

So what was this job that he told the police about—that he'd come home from to find her unconscious on the floor?

Had he gotten a job between June 23rd and July 3rd? Or was this another lie?

Maybe he had another plan for making money.

"You can take fifty thousand dollars out on someone without them even knowing," he'd said, minutes after informing me that my mother was dead.

Did he see their dire financial situation and think, *I could get a job, or I could murder my sister for insurance money...*

If his access to dangerous drugs was his means for murder, was money his motive?

The answer to this may be hiding in a phone call I had with my mother not long before she died.

His first thought in the morning:
the needle. The small plastic bag.
How to heat it. How to
get it into his veins.
Even with his shame, it's easier
to think of this than—

—excerpt of the poem "to the uncle who hit us" from the chapbook *Evolution*

CHAPTER FOUR

I don't remember the exact day or time my mother and I had the following conversation, but I do remember I was sitting outside when she called. Flagstones trace the mulch beds in my backyard, and sometimes I like to sit on the warm stones about thirty feet from the bird feeder, my bare feet in the grass, and watch the wildlife.

In the summertime my yard is overrun with cardinals, blue jays, finches, doves, robins, chipmunks, squirrels, and rabbits. Sometimes also deer and skunks. I also found a possum sleeping in the compost bin once.

This may or may not be because I put seed out for them and keep several watering stations clean and full.

I was doing just that, watching the birds flitter through the thick maple branches above, calling out to one another, when my phone rang.

And during the call, my mom whispered, "Joe looks like he got the *shit* beat out of him."

I was familiar with the whisper tactic. It meant he was

close, within earshot, and she had to watch what she said lest it trigger an argument.

"What do you mean?" I ask, teasing Charley with a blade of grass.

"His face is black and blue."

"Did he say what happened?"

"No."

"Ask him."

"I don't want to. It'll just piss him off. But it looks like he got the *shit* kicked out of him."

Buying or selling drugs probably doesn't bring you into contact with kumbaya people. Joe must run in rough circles.

But what had happened exactly? Was it simply a matter of a drug deal gone wrong? Did he say the wrong thing to the wrong person? Or was it more than that?

Was it possible that in addition to the unpaid utilities and mortgage, my uncle owes someone money? A *bad* someone?

Did they give him a little taste of that threat, maybe?

Did they threaten to end his life if he didn't pay up?

If a drug lord says give me X amount of money or I'll tear one of your eyes out, would you knock off your sister and collect the insurance policy posthaste?

Worse—would you knock off your mother *first*, and when that doesn't produce enough money, go after your sister too?

Because this isn't the first time I've wondered if maybe my grandmother's death wasn't accidental either. No one ever told me what her cause of death was. She'd had many heart attacks over the years, and at eighty-four, it seemed like she was on borrowed time as it was.

But it might not be a coincidence that my mother and grandmother died so close together.

I turn this conversation over in my mind as I sit in my yard again, but this time I'm not watching the birds. I'm barely aware of the low din of a car rolling down the street and something rustling in the grass. And this time I'm not talking on the phone to my mom. I'm texting Katie.

Please, God. Please don't let it be that he killed them for money. Let it be a mistake. Let it be that he really did get a job. That he really was trying to do better, and one night came home and found her and has a really, really good reason why he didn't call for help.

Maybe his story about heroin was just a panicked lie in the face of law enforcement.

Let it be COVID or her health. Let it be whatever was giving her seizures and memory loss.

To Katie, I write, *He told me she was worse off than I knew. That she was setting pans on fire because she'd leave them on the stove. That she was stuffing things in the freezer.*

If he did kill her for money...was this what he told himself to make it all right?

Is this how he justified it in his mind? Did he tell himself he was doing her a favor, putting her out of her misery? That *that* was the real reason she needed to go.

What was she putting in the freezer? Katie asks.

Remote or something?

Sounds like Tony's grandma. Her husband's grandmother had lived with them during the last stages of her dementia. *Why didn't he tell you about the fires?*

He said she didn't want me to worry.

Why the f*** wasn't he worried? she adds. *Better question: Why the hell was he leaving her alone if she was setting fires? That's some negligence right there.*

Negligence.

If so, maybe he hadn't wanted to kill her for money. Maybe he was simply tired of taking care of her and wanted her gone.

But wanting to do something and being capable of it aren't the same.

Do I think it's possible that my uncle could kill someone?

Accidentally—yes, of course. He's a violent person with little self-control. If he loses his temper, all bets are off. If he'd lost his temper with my mother that night, if they really had a fight about money, it's possible that he lost control and caused enough damage with his fists to end her life.

That would explain the "state of her room."

But cold, premeditated murder?

That suggests a much crueler, darker mind. This is where I keep getting stuck. This is the possibility that my mind is struggling to accept. That perhaps he is much more calculating than I realized.

That maybe he didn't move her body from the living room to the bedroom out of panic or fear, but according to his sinister plan. That maybe he didn't even come home and discover the scene but instead was present the entire time, watching death overtake her with a certain excited anticipation.

Then there's the rumor to consider.

Whispered at my grandfather's funeral, that Joe had "helped my grandfather along." That he'd taken it upon himself to end my grandfather's long-suffering battle against emphysema.

What did Joe stand to inherit when my grandfather died? Property and money.

There is a name for this, for a person who believes they are doing someone a favor by ending their life. To be clear, I'm not talking about qualified medical professionals who help consenting adults pass on. I'm talking about people who do not want to die—but are murdered anyway.

This sort of serial killer is called an angel of mercy.

Could Joe be an angel of mercy?

Does he view himself as the dutiful son and brother, willing to make the hard decisions no one else can?

Verbally, he often paints himself that way. When he talks about rescuing my mom from the hospital. When he talks about taking care of my grandmother, with such pride, as if he's never slammed his fists into her weathered face.

Is my uncle the sort of cold-blooded man who could let my mother lie unconscious on the floor as he tore her room apart looking for money?

Or perhaps there is a more damning clue.

A bizarre phone call.

On Friday July 3rd, at 10:10 a.m., almost exactly twenty-four hours before he would tell me he found my mother dead, I received a phone call.

Mom New Cell, it said.

When I answered, it was Joe.

I was surprised. Joe has never, *ever* called me before.

"Hello?"

"Here, talk to your momma," he said in his slow drawl. He sounded high to me. His voice thick.

There was a shuffle on the line, and then my mother said hello.

"Are you okay?" I asked her, trying to take measure of the situation.

She laughed. "I'm fine. Are *you* okay?"

"Joe called me, so I thought something was going on."

"No," she said. She sounded as confused as I was. "I'm fine, honey. Are you okay?"

Her voice was crystal clear. Absolutely lucid. No slurring. No confusion.

We went on like this for a few minutes, trying to figure

out why the call had been orchestrated. Finally we gave up, and I asked her what she had planned for the day. I asked about her health, her dogs.

"Fat, sassy, and spoiled," she told me.

She asked how my squash were doing.

"Terrible," I told her. "I think I have bugs."

"You sound better," I added later. "You don't sound as stressed as you did last time."

"Joe got a job," she told me. "Everything is going to be all right."

Then the call ended without fanfare.

This might not seem weird to you, I know.

But I keep turning this call over in my mind.

Again and again.

Why would Joe call me when he never had before? Not even to tell me my grandmother was dead and my mother hospitalized?

Why, of *all* the times this one anomaly of a call could have happened, it happens hours before my mother's death?

Could it really just be coincidence?

Or did Joe know what he had planned for that night?

And he wanted to make sure we—my mother and I—had one last chance to say goodbye.

Imagine wide boulevards, empty.
Birds, if there are
still birds, will darken the sky.
They will be the ones who remember
our songs, our stories.
When the world has ended,
when the world has moved on,
what will be left of us?

—excerpt of the poem "cloud gate" from the collection *Birds and Other Dreamers*

CHAPTER FIVE

I can't bear to wait anymore. I call Detective Barnes to ask about the results of the autopsy.

As the phone rings—seemingly for an eternity—my heart starts pounding. My palms are sweating.

I want him to answer and tell me it's a mistake.

I want him to say that my mother's death was something simple and unproblematic. COVID-19, or a heart attack, or anything but a tragic end to my mother's tragic life.

Anything but one of the awful scenarios I've concocted in my dark mind.

I'm praying, not for the last time, that my uncle is innocent.

The ringing stops. A voice says, "Detective Barnes."

"Hi, it's me. Kory. Leitha's daughter. I'm sorry to bother you—I'm sure you're really busy—but I'm hoping you have my mother's autopsy results."

"Oh hi, Kory, yes. I was just about to call you."

I finally have the detective on the phone and I can

barely hear him. The pounding in my ears drowns out his words.

"I'm sorry," I tell the detective. "Can you say that again?"

"We didn't find anything."

"What do you mean, you didn't find anything?"

"There's no damage to her body. Well, she has a scratch on her right arm, but it isn't considerable. Maybe he pushed her down. There are a few bruises, but it's hard to tell how old bruises are. And there's a place on her scalp that was bleeding underneath, but that could've happened if she'd collapsed. There's nothing that points to a clear cause of death."

A wave of relief washes through me.

I didn't realize until this moment how afraid I'd been that he'd beaten her to death. That her final moments were full of terror and pain.

But that isn't what happened. He didn't do it with his fists, and for some reason, that's marginally better.

"So…it wasn't a violent death?" I ask, knowing my disbelief must be showing.

The detective sounds like a good guy. At the very least, he's incredibly patient with me. "No, ma'am. There's nothing to suggest he strangled her, or hit her. Even the bruises are of varying ages, so it's hard to say if a struggle caused those."

My mother and I are the same in that we perpetually mis-measure the width of doorways. All my life she'd clipped door frames with an elbow or shoulder and would have a bruise dark enough to have you believing someone took a bat to her.

The detective goes on. "The X-ray found no evidence of an air bubble. There were no needle marks anywhere on her body."

I stop him here. "No needle marks at all?"

"No, ma'am."

Of course, it's possible that they missed something small, like a puncture between the toes, but he assures me they checked everywhere and were very thorough.

If there are no track marks, then she wasn't a secret heroin addict. It means my mom was probably telling the truth about being clean.

I remind the detective of this. "She wasn't doing heroin. He lied when he said she'd used heroin."

"Yes, ma'am, seems so."

"Do you think he gave her drugs? Or poisoned her?"

"Unfortunately, we won't know that until the tox screen comes back."

"How long will that take?"

"At least eight weeks."

In truth, it will take over fourteen.

I'm dreading the wait. How do I endure months of not knowing whether or not he killed her?

I realize instantly that if there's no proof from her body that he killed her, the only thing holding him in jail is the warrant.

"What will happen to Joe?" I ask.

"Yes, ma'am, when we arrested him we found heroin and meth inside his body."

Inside his body, Katie would later repeat back to me. *He's a guy, so we're talking about the butt, right?*

Never one to mince words, my friend.

The fact that Joe was arrested with heroin and meth "inside his body" and that my mother had not so much as a single puncture wound tells me that his story about her breaking into the safe and stealing his heroin is bogus. It was a lie, and he knew it was a lie.

But why did Joe tell it?

Why insist that it was heroin when it could've been any of the drugs he had in the safe? We know he had at least my mother's prescriptions, heroin, and meth inside. Probably others. He could've told them anything. That she took meth. That she took too many pills.

But he'd said heroin.

Why had he insisted that it was the least likely of all? Unless he knew what the tox screen would say. Unless he *knew* because he'd given it to her?

"If it comes back that she has heroin in her system," I tell the detective, "you know this means he used it to kill her. He was the user with track marks. Not her."

Detective Barnes placates me with a respectful "Yes, ma'am."

And the fact that there is no fatal damage to her body tells me that he didn't lose control of himself. It wasn't like he lost his patience and struck her.

This isn't the ashtray incident of 2006.

If he killed her, it was a calculated decision. Maybe even something he planned far in advance.

I tell the detective about the insurance policy. Tell him, "On the morning he called to tell me she was dead, he asked if I had an insurance policy on her. He said you can take fifty thousand dollars out on someone without them even knowing, which I thought was a very specific amount of money. Is there a way for you to check and see if there's a policy?"

"Yes, ma'am, I could check."

Good, I think. Because if there is a policy and Joe is named as the beneficiary, that would explain some things. For better or worse.

When I check Joe's booking that afternoon, I see that he had a court date for August 5th, the day after his fifty-second birthday.

There's the strangulation charge and the two new drug charges.

I wonder how much time he'll get for the drug charges or the strangulation. I'm not confident, given his track record, that he'll get much at all. Maybe as little as ninety days or possibly a year.

"Why don't you think the drug charges will stick? " my wife asks when I fill her in on the autopsy update and the long, uncertain wait stretching before me. "Has he gotten out of jail time before?"

"Yes." I laugh. "A lot."

When I look more closely at his booking, there are the three pending charges. The outstanding strangulation charge and the two drugs charges: the first, contraband in a penal institution—intoxicant/contraband substance, listed as a felony; and the second, a contraband substance possession or casual exchange, listed as a misdemeanor.

Between the heroin and the meth, I don't know which is a felony and which is a misdemeanor, so who knows what the authorities think is worse. It probably has something to do with quantity, but the detective didn't tell me how much he had on him.

I don't stop at the recent charges, though. I search the archives as well.

Including the three new pending offenses, I find that my uncle has 117 charges in Davidson County alone.

One *hundred* and *seventeen*.

It seems his extensive life of crime began—on record, anyway—in 1987, when he was found guilty of burglary, forced entry of a non-residential property. He would've been nineteen at the time. He certainly didn't slow down between then and now.

Of the 117 charges, several of them have the same dates and judge, so I assume they are incidents that occurred at the same time.

Regardless, the arrest record is thirty-two pages long when I print it from my computer.

As I comb the information, trying to decipher and organize it, one thing becomes abundantly clear:

My uncle Joe is one lucky guy.

Outright, over sixty of the charges have been dismissed, retired, closed, or deemed nolle prosequi, which turns out is a fancy way of saying the court decided to abandon the case.

The times where he *was* found guilty of crime, in nearly every instance, the worst offense was dismissed and substituted for a lesser charge.

For example, in April 2001, when he attempted to choke me, he was charged with domestic violence/assault with bodily injury. But this was thrown out and he was convicted instead of harassment. This misdemeanor came with a sentence of eleven months and twenty-nine days in jail.

Did he go to jail?

Only for thirty days. The rest of his sentence was suspended.

That is the pattern I see over and over again in his record: Dismissed or reduced crime. Suspended or shortened sentence.

November 1995—assault bodily injury—dismissed
June 1997—aggravated assault—intentionally/knowingly—nolle prosequi
March 1999—aggravated assault—intentionally/knowingly—dismissed
February 2006—assault domestic bodily injury—dismissed

June 2007—assault, domestic bodily injury—dismissed
May 2016—assault, domestic bodily injury—dismissed

A few times the system halfheartedly pursued justice. In September 2004, he was convicted guilty after trial of assault, domestic bodily injury and sentenced to nine months, though he served only ninety days.

In August 2015, he was convicted of assault domestic bodily injury for the second time, but this eleven-month, twenty-nine-day sentence was suspended for all but sixty days. He was convicted of assault domestic bodily injury for a third time and given another nine months in May 2017.

Do I even need to tell you this nine-month sentence was suspended completely in lieu of probation?

Assuming I'm reading this record correctly—and it's a shame they don't teach us how to read criminal records in school—I can find only one exception to this pattern where the felony charge stuck instead of being replaced with a misdemeanor.

In October 2008, he was convicted of aggravated assault with a deadly weapon—intentionally/knowingly.

He was sentenced to four years in the Davidson County Sheriff's Facility. However, there is a "yes" beside "suspended," so we might assume he was only given the supervised probation for these four years and never served any actual jail time for the felony.

These are only the assault charges.

Over the years he was also charged with theft, burglary, robbery, and carjacking. There were DUIs in August 1993, February 1995, June 1995, July 1998, and September 1998. Public intoxication in 2003. Criminal impersonation in July 2001 and November 2007.

We're not even to page ten of thirty-two.

He's also been charged with contributing to the delinquency of a minor, child abuse, child endangerment, disturbing the peace, disorderly conduct, stalking, and harassment.

His favorite crimes—or at least the crimes he repeated the most—are driving on a revoked or suspended license, criminal trespassing, evading or resisting arrest, and leaving the scene of an accident, with or without injured persons present.

I don't bother counting up all the drug charges: possession, possession with intent to sell, contraband in a penal institution, legend drug possession, and habitual offender.

The drug charges paint a more complete picture of his chronic addiction problems, but it doesn't tell me if he's capable of murder.

It does, however, suggest that he might not have feared consequences for his actions.

Why would he? If every time he was up for a felony charge it was reduced to a misdemeanor, or dropped altogether?

If every time he should've gone to jail for years, he instead got probation, how in the world would he have thought his actions would have lasting consequences?

And given the overlapping in the charges, he must've defaulted on his probation several times. Is there no penalty for violating probation?

If so, why were they so willing to cut him so much slack?

Because he's white? If he was black, the first drug charge would've been enough to send him to *prison*, not jail, for a long time.

Is he a narc for Nashville's drug department?

Or could my uncle Joe really be so charismatic in a courtroom?

He would've learned the value of such a facade at my grandmother's knee. As a traveling pastor, she taught him how to present himself as a good Christian man whenever it suited the situation, regardless of whether or not his actions supported such ideologies.

Had my uncle stood in front of judge after judge and painted himself as a harmless addict with a problem? A misunderstood but ultimately good Christian man?

Let's say we overlook the drug charges altogether. I personally have issues with the criminalization of drugs, as it only upholds the school-to-prison pipeline used to incarcerate and enslave black Americans.

And there are good people who suffer from addiction.

But even without the drug charges, I don't understand why no one has taken his history of violence seriously.

How in the world can this system expect a man like my uncle Joe to stop putting his hands on people when he receives little to no consequences for repeatedly doing so?

Notably, there was no arrest record for the ashtray incident in 2006.

I'm sorry, but if a man fractures someone's skull and causes internal brain bleeding so bad that emergency surgery is needed to keep that blood from flooding the victim's brain and causing death, he's merited some serious jail time.

Yet there wasn't even an assault charge for that.

The police went to the house to investigate. An ambulance was called to collect my mother's unconscious body. It wasn't like no one was informed.

So why weren't charges pressed?

Why did they leave that burden of defending herself to my mother?

My mother was in the hospital with sixty-plus staples in the shape of a fishhook on the left side of her head.

She'd forgotten how to speak. How to walk.

How, exactly, did anyone expect her to press charges?

No matter how you slice it, 117 offenses is a lot—someone shouldn't even have the opportunity to accrue 117 charges on a record.

And let's not forget that the most recent act of violence against my mother was the February 2019 strangulation.

This matters because a 2008 study published in the *Journal of Emergency Medicine*[1] says that 43% of women who were murdered by domestic assault and 45% of victims of attempted murder had been strangled by their assailant within the year before.

Domestic violence strangulation has become such a significant predictor of attempted and successful murder that police departments across the country have begun to take it more seriously.

Even non-deadly strangulation shows that the assailant isn't against the idea of killing their victim.

There's one fact about all of this that I find the most infuriating.

Had the police department committed to arresting and charging Joe with strangulation in February 2019, committed to making him serve at least two years for that charge, without substituting it for a shorter sentence or probation—my uncle would've still been in jail come July 2020.

My mother might still be alive.

We're given bodies and the agency
to sleep, wake, and dream.
But what of the orbit?
The gravity of the collapsed star
in our chests, the oppressive power of
all that wing-pins us in place?

—excerpt of the poem "the theory of us" from the
collection *You Can't Keep It*

CHAPTER SIX

The day I called the police to report that my mother was in the bathroom, terrified and strangled, was also the day I let Joe convince me it didn't happen.

There were hours between the phone call and the gaslighting, of course. He had to escape my grandmother's house, evade the police, and then come back later once the coast was clear.

So it was later in the evening when he had my mother call me.

In this call he explained that I'd gotten it all wrong. That my mother, in the throes of her psychosis, had attacked him first.

It didn't help that my mother no longer sounded cogent on the phone.

She wasn't consumed by the fear that gripped her earlier in the day. Her focus was gone.

To him, I said, "She told me that you strangled her."

When he repeated this to her, she said, "She's lying. Joe, she's lying."

And began to cry.

Here, to my shame, I did wonder if I'd gotten it wrong.

As she cried, she spoke about my father.

"I went through hell for her," she tells him. "I went through hell so she would have a dad."

Joe said, "That happened a long time ago."

But she didn't seem to hear this. She was slipping away from us.

Into the silence, Joe said, "She isn't well, Kory. Surely you can hear that." Before I could answer, he added, "Don't call the police no more. We handle our business in the family."

It wasn't like I didn't know my mother was far from innocent. She'd put me through hell more times than I could count.

When she was drunk, she could be mean. Even violent. She could slap and kick and bite. And while she'd never hurt me, I'd been witness to plenty of spats. Her first line of defense was always a good shove, her way of telling someone to back off, and that was my cue to jump in. To speak softly to her and try to de-escalate the situation. Sometimes it worked.

Sometimes it didn't.

This was the mother Joe wanted me to remember, to think of now. He was counting on twenty-five years of bad experiences to overshadow what was happening in that house now. That night.

He wanted me to forget that *now* my mom was too sick to act as she had before.

My mother was no longer the feisty drunk of her twenties who could kick and scream if the police tried to shove her in the back of the police car. By February 2019 she was fifty-five years old, and the hep C she'd contracted decades earlier had left her body ravaged with chronic fatigue, muscle weakness, and constant nausea. She got winded easily, just walking down to the mailbox or when taking her dogs outside.

More importantly, she didn't drink anymore. She hadn't for years.

This is what he does, you see.

He twists a story, takes a litany of half-truths and turns them first in the light, then in the darkness, until you can't be sure what you're looking at. For someone like me, who makes sense out of the insane world by clinging to facts like flotsam, it's a hell of a mind game. Well played.

But here are the facts:

Keeping things in the family only ever serves to protect the *abuser*—never the abused.

That's a fact.

He *is* the abuser.

He is much bigger than my mother. At least six or seven inches taller. And far stronger. He doesn't have her health problems, or her physical weakness.

He could've pushed her back or restrained her for her safety. He could've tried talking to her, or asking me to calm her down.

He could've locked her in a room.

No matter how angry she might have made him, he could've done a dozen other things in that moment to stop her from hitting him or hurting herself.

I know because I've been him.

I've had to make these choices. My mother has been uncontrollable as a mad dog, and yet I've never had to put my hands on her.

If I could manage it, being even two inches shorter than my mother, so could he.

Yet he strangled her.

He used intense and sustained compression on her throat until she had dark, visible bruising.

The police saw this. Recorded it down. They had enough evidence to issue the warrant for his arrest.

These are the facts.

I shouldn't have let him convince me otherwise.

Joe didn't beat my mother to death. I say this to myself on a loop in the days following the preliminary autopsy results.

At least he didn't beat her. It could've been so much worse. She could've been unrecognizable. He could've buried her somewhere and said she ran away. That she took off with a guy. He could've done so many things.

Of course, there is a harder, more unforgiving part of me who is quick to say, *Kory, she's still dead. And if it really was an overdose, he would've known what that was when it was happening and he let it happen.*

I know this voice. She's been with me a long time.

I picture this version of me in dramatic armor with a flaming sword and eyes full of hellfire. Sometimes with black wings flowing down her back.

I honestly can't tell if she's an angel or a demon. But she's dressed like this because she's always ready to do battle. She is, in fact, the reason why sometimes I have *no chill*.

But on the upside, I know that anytime the pain comes, anytime I stay down too long, she will show up, and in a tone that brooks no argument, she'll drag me to my fight.

She'll draw from impossible, seemingly bottomless wells of strength that I'm always surprised to find that I have.

How can I keep going? Truly? How in the hell do I keep doing this? And yet—

You can do this. You just need to get on top of it.
Get up.

Why am I talking about this imaginary friend?

Because this is who *I'm* doing battle with now. In the wake of my mother's death, in the face of a loss I've never suffered before, this hardass has shown up.

She wants me to push through, to armor up as I always do when my heart is breaking.

But the funny thing about a death is it shakes everything loose. Even things you thought would never change begin to shift.

When someone you love dies, you simply can't do what you've always done.

I don't know why, but it doesn't work anymore. Losing my mother stops me.

It stops everything.

This is the first time I've wanted to fight *for* my grief rather than against it.

I feel myself digging in. Becoming obstinate. I'm demanding my right to feel all this hurt.

I'm thinking things like, *You took my mother, but you're not going to take this too, you son of a bitch.*

I'm not even sure who I'm mad at. My uncle? The world?

Myself?

I flip through my mother's photographs, remembering hard times and good times.

I'm deliberately ignoring all of its demands:

Get up. You have a business to run and books to write. Hell, you have a house to clean. Stop crying. You have work to do.

It doesn't help that people don't like it when you're depressed. It makes them uncomfortable. I can see it in my wife's face. She doesn't know what to say, what to do for me. She's tiptoeing around the edge of my grief, trying to ride the waves as one minute I'm okay and the next I'm not.

Hardass uses this as ammunition.

See, you're making it worse. And you're stronger than this. It's not like you didn't know this was coming.

Who cares if I knew she was going to die? It doesn't make it less sad.

Get up.

No. I'm petulant as I lift another photograph from the pile and pull another tissue from the box. *If your mother being murdered isn't reason enough to be sad, then I don't know what the hell is.*

I'm reminded again that it isn't only my mother that I'm mourning. It's every hope and dream I had for her.

I used to dream that one day I'd be rich, and that when I was I could afford to buy my mom her own house, somewhere nice and safe, and far away from Joe. That I could afford to take care of her, pay her bills, have a full-time aide or nurse to look after her and make sure she took all her medicines correctly. Someone to take her places and make sure she had fun. Someone to keep me updated on her situation at all times. To make sure she wanted for nothing, and knew how much I loved her. Most importantly, I would be able to visit her more.

But those dreams are sinking like stones thrown.

And dreams aren't the only things unraveling.

There are things I've carried all my life—coping mechanisms and reflexes—that are beginning to feel outdated.

Hardass is great when it comes to persistence, resilience, or motivation.

But the truth is that Hardass hasn't always helped me. She's kept me safe, kept me going.

Yet sometimes I've also pushed back against people who only want to help me. My responses to a challenge or a difficult moment can be more aggressive than they need to be.

When I don't like something, when I want to change something, I can be brutal.

And what has that ever gotten me?

I'm beginning to imagine a new, terrifying possibility.

I could be gentle.

Not only with others, but with myself. That maybe this is long overdue.

Of course, I get immediate pushback.

Gentle? Are you kidding me? This world isn't gentle. People aren't gentle. It's going to hurt like hell.

The world isn't gentle? Maybe that's the problem.

We aren't as kind as we could be. Especially not with ourselves.

But grief requires a gentle hand.

A soft place to fall, to rest.

I realize that now, as I lie on my own blanket of grief, my face swollen and voice thick.

I need gentle. I just don't know how to do it. Yet.

My belligerent moping is interrupted by a call from the medical examiner's office.

"Yes, ma'am, we're calling to ask you for details about your mother's arrangement."

My mother's arrangement.

Right. Because there's still the matter of her body.

"Oh, sorry," I begin. "I didn't realize she was....was ready. Are you sure? My mother wants—wanted—to be cremated. I didn't think I could do that before the investigation was over."

"Yes, ma'am. Dr. Wright took all the necessary samples. We have what we need. Your mother is ready to be discharged to you. We just don't have the name of the funeral home you'd like us to release her to."

You might think I'm a moron, but this is actually the first time I realize I'm going to have to make funeral arrangements.

"Did you have a funeral home in mind?" the woman on the phone asks.

"Uh, no. No. I don't."

I've never buried anyone and I feel like it shows. Even with my two dogs who passed, the veterinarian took the bodies away and gave me back the ashes. I hadn't had to do anything. They just called me when it was all finished. Then I went to the office to pick the ashes up—which had, disturbingly, been put in a gift bag.

That was it.

I take a deep breath. "Do you recommend a particular funeral home or…?"

"We aren't allowed to do that, ma'am," she says. "But I can send you the list of places you can call."

"Do you have any idea how much a cremation costs in Tennessee?"

Like everyone else in the pandemic, I'm trying to watch where my money is going. I've heard burials are ridiculously expensive, but have no idea how much a cremation costs.

"I can include the number to social services. If your mother qualifies, they cover the burial costs."

"Oh. Yes. Thank you. Oh, one more thing."

"Yes, ma'am."

"My mother had a cross that she always wore. Do you have that? If so, can it be mailed to me? I'm happy to pay for shipping."

Because I'd bought my mother that cross for Mother's Day a couple years ago and wanted it back if possible.

"Let me check on that for you."

Silence on the line.

While she's gone, I get an email alert on my computer and check it. It's the list of funeral homes as well as the number to the social services office.

Then, "Ma'am, there was no jewelry on the body when it came in."

"None at all?" I ask, my blood icing.

"No, ma'am."

I think again of what the detective vaguely referred to as "the state of her room" on the morning he found her. When I'd asked for clarification, he'd said it looked like things had been thrown around, like maybe there was a fight.

This tracks with Joe's story that they'd had a fight about money.

Though it wasn't like my mother had much of value.

Clothes.

Her TV and bed.

When Joe had called to tell me my mother passed, he'd offered to send me her belongings.

The only possessions I could think of—the books I'd signed and sent her, the stories, unpublished, that she'd kept for me, things I'd written while in school, an abundance of photographs—were sentimental but not worth much.

The possibility Joe would actually box this stuff up and send it to me was slim.

When he'd offered to do that, I'd asked about the necklace.

This necklace wasn't extravagant. I think it cost me about $150. It's not like it came from Tiffany's. But it was pretty and she'd worn it every day.

When I asked Joe about it on the morning of her

death, telling him to please to look for it, he'd said, "I think I know where that is."

Then proceeded to describe it perfectly. The delicate gold strand. The small diamond set in the gold at the center where the two bars crossed.

"I'll look around for it," he said, as if it could be anywhere but my mother's neck.

I assumed he didn't have a chance to do this, since he ended his call with me when the police arrived.

When I ask the morgue attendant to double-check if she was brought in with any jewelry and she says no again, I'm left with only question:

Did Joe wait until my mother stopped breathing to take it off her neck?

The water droplets echo in the metal basin
like the ticking of a clock,
the minutes between *now* and *dinnertime*, my
impatience for the sound of your key in the door.

—excerpt of the poem "Timberlane Street" from the chapbook *Evolution*

CHAPTER SEVEN

Several calls back and forth with the social services offices lead me to discover that my mother does in fact qualify for a cremation service. The fact that her income was only $795 makes this possible. I'm grateful. Between calls, I go through the helpful list of funeral homes, and even the cheapest cremation is $900 plus the cost to ship her to me. Most run north of $1,500.

Though cumbersome, I am still grateful to fill out the lengthy application for the assistance. I provide all the information about her and her parents that I can recall, but there's a snag. They've gotten her age wrong—it was probably Joe who misinformed them—and this technicality holds everything up. The paperwork has to be redone. They're very particular about making sure it's the right body that's getting cremated.

I appreciate this. I want to receive my mom, after all. Not someone's grandpa.

Yet due to the confusion, my mother's body ends up being in the cooler at the medical examiner's office for almost a month before it's finally released to the funeral home that agreed to do the cremation at the state's affixed price.

One pain point for me in all of this is the matter of my mother's disability check. Her mental condition required that she have a guardian, a responsible person that received her money on her behalf and spent it appropriately on my mother's needs. This had been my grandmother when she was alive, and when she died just four months before my mother did, the official caregiver had to be reassigned, which apparently they did without fanfare.

They put my uncle—of all people—in charge of my mother's well-being without so much as a background check.

She told me about how they went down to the SSI office, proved who he was and let him fill out the paperwork.

That was it. They put his name on her money just like that.

Why didn't anyone check his arrest record, his history of violence against her, before giving him control of her money? Why hadn't someone come to the house and inspected their living situation?

Surely, if someone had looked closely, they would have realized it wasn't safe to give a violent addict control of his sister's money. That her housing situation was dire with the unpaid mortgage and utilities.

A background check and home visit isn't expecting too much. I had to do a ten-page application, with references, *and* a home visit just to adopt my dog.

I would expect at least as much for a human life.

It's true families like mine are complicated and the system puts a lot of the burden of caretaking on families who are not equipped or capable of that caretaking.

It wasn't that I didn't love my mother. It wasn't that I

hadn't tried nearly everything to secure her well-being and happiness.

It's that everything about my mother's psychosis and caregiving would have destroyed me. This life I worked so hard to create would've fallen apart.

My wife loves me. But she isn't built to endure what my mother would've done to our lives if I'd tried to move my mom to Michigan and had assumed full-time care of her.

Don't get me wrong, I am a resilient person. I'm even a fully functional adult most of the time. But I have managed to overcome much of my trauma for one reason: I self-care like it's an Olympic sport.

I'm not kidding. I spend more time on self-care than Michael Phelps spends in a pool.

I exercise most days. I watch how much sugar I eat because it makes my moods go too high or too low. I won't get out of bed unless I've had eight or nine hours of sleep, even if this means snoozing on and off until almost noon. I make time for friends and for reading. For writing and journaling and doing things I love like painting. I meditate every day for thirty minutes and drink only water and tea and very rarely coffee because it makes me jittery or triggers migraines.

I walk my dog. I get fresh air.

It takes so much time and work for me just to care for myself and to be a good, healthy, present person for the people I love—how in the world would I have also taken care of someone like my mother?

It took me fifteen years of fighting tooth and nail to get to where I am now, in a place where I can take care of myself like this.

We don't live in a society that allows this. I had to break a lot of rules to make this happen.

It was necessary to rearrange my career and schedule.

Still, this is a privilege most people don't have.

People like my mother need care, but they can't get it from their own broken homes.

What that will get you is two sick and miserable people. Nothing else.

I'm worried this might sound like "Lock her up in an asylum!" Because those are the only sorts of places that I imagine we have now for someone who needs the level of support my mother needed.

But, no, locking her away somewhere wouldn't have helped her.

Treating her like a dirty secret would've only ensured she never got well again.

And I know that the solutions aren't easy and we might not have them all yet.

We simply don't have the mental health infrastructure we need in America. Places and spaces for people to move away from their toxic environments to heal their unresolved traumas, to whatever degree they're capable of. A place for people to heal where they feel free rather than confined. Supported rather than judged.

I might have dreamed about the day I would have the money to throw at this problem, to give my mother something better. But my chance has passed.

I know people *are* trying. Changes *have been* made.

It's just so hard to look at all that's *not* been done and feel anything less than exhaustion at what still needs to be accomplished.

But I can hope. I can believe that one day we will make something better.

I don't know my mother's full medical record. And I don't know exactly what part of her record qualified her for disability. I'd been told that she was diagnosed with manic depression by the time I was seven or eight. If you haven't heard of manic depression, it's because now we call it bipolar disorder. By today's standards she would be classified as bipolar I—distinguished from bipolar II by her extensive manic episodes.

I don't know if this diagnosis was accurate. When later discussing it with a psychiatrist, she said it sounded more like borderline personality disorder to her when considering how fast my mother could experience a mental shift. And Seroquel, one of my mother's medications, is given to people with borderline personality disorder as well, so it's possible she was rediagnosed later after another evaluation. I do know that at one point they added schizoaffective disorder to her charts, also treated with Seroquel. The difference between schizophrenia and schizoaffective disorder is the presence of the mood disorder. Schizophrenia may or may not show symptoms of mood disorder, but with schizoaffective disorder, it's front and center, and episodes can be triggered by stress, such as a death.

Regardless of which diagnosis fits better, I can think of two good examples that illustrate my mother's swings.

One happened when I was fifteen.

Shay, my mom's girlfriend at the time, was driving her cool green Mustang. She had the bass turned up so that the backseat rattled. I loved it.

My mom was in the passenger seat, singing along with the radio. Cracking jokes.

She could be funny when she wanted to be, my mother. She had a fantastic, sarcastic wit that I loved.

On this night, I don't remember about what, but she had us rolling.

We'd just had a nice dinner—probably McDonald's or

Taco Bell—something fancier than our usual dollar store Hamburger Helper fare.

I was in the backseat, laughing so hard I had tears in my eyes. I looked out the window, seeing the streetlights streak by. I remember being happy.

Then came the shift.

Shay screamed, "Leitha, no! Leitha, *come on!*"

The car jerked.

I turned away from the window in time to see my mother hit Shay in the side of her head. Once, twice. She was trying to grab her hair and pull.

She was crying.

Two seconds ago we were laughing, having a good time. Now my mother was crying with tears streaming down her face.

Shay was trying to drive with one hand and protect her head with the other. "Leitha, stop!"

"Hey!" I screamed. "We're on the road!"

The car jerked again.

We traveled across the median as a car swerved then honked long and loud.

"Christ!" I swore from the backseat, now scrambling for my seatbelt, trying to find the buckle with shaking hands.

I was convinced we were going to crash, and alarm bells in my head were yelling in a mock spaceship voice, *Prepare for impact.*

Shay slammed on the brakes and the car came to a screeching halt in the middle of the road.

The car behind us whipped around, more honking. Someone was swearing with their middle finger out the window.

I gave up on getting my seatbelt buckled and instead

reach around the seat, grabbing my mother and trying to pin her against it.

Shay managed to get us onto the shoulder before we were killed.

At first my mom resisted my hold, until I said, "Mom, no. Stop it. Just stop."

And she stopped.

She went soft against the seat while I whispered, "It's okay. Mom, it's okay. Just breathe. Breathe."

I held her even after she began to cry in earnest. I told her I loved her.

I kept telling her everything would be okay.

Once, when I was in third grade, I was in a musical. Nothing special. We were little kids and the expectations were low, which is good because despite my thick curly hair, I'm no Shirley Temple.

But I was excited because my mother was going to come see me sing in my little costume up on the stage, which had been erected in our lunchroom, against one wall, with the plastic chairs we usually sat in during meals arranged in makeshift rows.

My mother was very excited about it. All day she kept bringing it up, singing my songs with me, helping me to memorize the lyrics. Her enthusiasm was contagious. All my nervousness evaporated in the deluge of her encouragement.

Since we were to rehearse for the concert one more time after school, I didn't expect to see her again until the performance.

"You'll be amazing, baby!" she told me as she kissed me that morning before I began my walk to school. "I'll be cheering the loudest! You won't miss me!"

Before the show began, I stood on the stage with the other kids, searching the crowd for her face, trying to find her among the sea of parents chatting before the show. Parents waving, parents cheering, parents taking their seats.

Then the lights went down, and I had to focus on not sounding like a strangled goose.

Then the show was over, and I ran off the stage, pumped to find my mom and what I assumed would be a rain shower of praise.

But as each child found their parents, as hair was ruffled and costumes straightened, as the pictures began, I kept searching.

I weaved my way through our little cafeteria, looking up into each friendly but strange face.

She wasn't there.

The only adult I knew was my teacher. And I ran to her the way a child does when she realizes she's lost. In the wrong place, and possibly forgotten.

"Ms. Weatherbee, I can't find my mom." Now I was close to tears, and I'm sure she could see that.

"Let's go look outside, sweetie. Some of the parents are outside smoking."

And while my mother did smoke, she wasn't outside in the congregation at the edge of the parking lot.

In fact, after all the parents cleared out, it was only me and Ms. Weatherbee in the cafeteria, surrounded by papier-mâché decorations, long after everyone else had gone home.

The police arrived first and collected me.

They tried to assure me they were looking for my mom. Not to worry, I was safe. I said nothing.

After the police car rolled up outside our little two-bedroom trailer that we shared with Shay, they found the house locked. The windows dark.

I said nothing as they broke in and brought me inside. These officers in uniform crowded the living room as I brushed my teeth, my hair. I changed into my pajamas and threw my book bag on the floor, homework forgotten.

As the hours passed, they kept insisting I could go to bed and sleep, with me insisting that I couldn't possibly until my mom came home.

It was almost midnight before one said, "Hey, honey, did you eat dinner?"

I hadn't. Nothing since lunch at school.

They stayed with me until Shay's second shift at the factory ended and she could come home.

But my mother was harder to track down.

They eventually found her car in a ditch, forty-five miles away.

While I was at school, her mood had turned. The mania I'd basked in that morning had swung into depression. Sometimes it did this on its own. Sometimes when a pill wore off or she'd begun to drink.

And that's what happened that night.

As I was singing "There's a Little Wheel A-Turning in My Heart," with glitter on my cheeks and an oversized scrunchy in my hair, my mother climbed behind the wheel of her car and drove off into the night, trying to put as much distance between herself and her life as she could.

After her death, I spoke to my grandmother
more than I had in years...
I'm sorry I let all that keep me away, I say.
And in her voice: *There's nothing left to forgive.*

—excerpt of the poem "amends" from the chapbook *Evolution*

CHAPTER EIGHT

My mother's body is still chilling in the medical examiner's freezer when Katie asks me what I'm going to do about her estate.

"She doesn't have anything," I tell her.

I review the list of meager possessions I wish Joe would send and know he will not. My stories, books, photographs. The cross necklace.

But there's no car. Nothing that could be called an *asset*. There was her dog, Biscuit, but it was taken along with the other two, Willow and Stella, to animal control the same day Joe was arrested and her body was carted off to the morgue.

"If she has anything," I say, "it's probably debt."

"Let me do a search. You never know," Katie offers. I would think she's tired of doing research, as often as she's required to do it for her work, but I appreciate her generosity nonetheless.

Not long after she texts me a single, ominous, *Uhhhh…*

Uhhh, what?

A second text comes through. For a moment, I'm not sure what I'm looking at.

Map & parcel. My mother's address.

And my grandmother's name and mother's name printed beside *Current Owner*.

What is this? I ask her, my thumb furiously working over the screen of my phone. *What am I looking at?*

It's the property record for the house, your grandmother's house.

But it only has Nana's name and my mother's name. I admit I sound a little dumbstruck to myself. *Where is Joe's name?*

She sends a second text with a quitclaim deed from 2008, when Joe did "hereby bargain, sell, remise, release, quitclaim and convey unto my grandmother all of his interest in the estate."

Am I reading this right? I ask her. *Does this house belong to my mom? Oh god, is this my house?*

Two seconds ago, I was lamenting not getting a box of photographs, and now I have to deal with the real possibility that my mother has an actual estate which I need to resolve. I've heard horror stories about probates and lawyer fees. About how it can take years to settle such loose ends in the courts and get everything squared away.

Nothing about this sounds appealing to me.

"But if you sell the house, you can pay off your student loans," my wife reminds me.

Ah, the small glimmer of hope.

Until I remember the mortgage.

"Wait. I don't think they've paid the mortgage since my grandmother died. Does that mean it's *my* mortgage now? Am *I* defaulting on a mortgage right now?" It takes a few minutes more to search the property record. It shows that the property taxes were paid by a bank in Michigan. I take down their name and number. After making a sandwich, I give them a call.

I try to explain who I am, the situation with the house, and why my uncle can't call them. But they can't tell me anything about the mortgage. It's in my grandmother's name and my uncle Joe is the only listed contact point.

"She's dead," I tell them. "She isn't going to pay anything. And he might not get out of jail for years."

"Ma'am, if that's true and you're to inherit the house, you will need to make a payment on the house in order to keep the loan from defaulting."

"A payment? You haven't even told me what the payment amounts are. Am I supposed to guess what the payment is? A hundred dollars? Five hundred?"

"No, ma'am, you have to make a full payment."

"And a full payment would be?"

Silence echoes on the line.

I take a deep breath. "All right. What do I have to do to gain access to this account?"

"We need death certificates for your grandmother and mother. Or if the court appoints you as the executor, we can tell you that information then. Or if you find a bill, the account information will be on that."

If I find a bill, as if I'm going to drive from Michigan to Tennessee and root around in the house. A new possibility shivers through me.

"A bill," I say. "Would it show how much is owed and what the minimum payment is?"

"Yes, ma'am."

I try to imagine returning to the house I haven't seen since I drove away in 2005, leaving my mother at the end of the driveway with her garbage bag of clothes and all my dreams of a fresh start dashed like a beer bottle on the concrete.

I look at the property record photo again. Then at Zillow, and Google Maps. The latest photo was taken by

Google in March 2019, within weeks of my mother being strangled. The house is how I remember it.

A single-story brick ranch house, with its white door and shutters. Chipped metal railings in a front garden bed as well as along one side of the concrete steps. In the photo, the front door is open, and I strain to see inside, for a face or maybe even a glimpse of my mother smoking a cigarette.

But the glass reflects only streaked blue light, the bright sky shimmering on its surface.

The large maple I loved to climb as a child stands proudly erect in the front yard, though its limbs are still bare. I remember tumbling down the slope, rolling and laughing until I flopped to stop in the ditch, where I picked sickly sweet purple irises running along the roadside.

How when the hard summer rains came I would run out into the storm, singing, twirling with my arms out, splashing in the puddles collecting on the concrete patio and howling like a wolf—until my exasperated grandmother came out with a towel and dragged me inside.

There is one difference in the photo that varies from my memories.

Behind the house sits a standing three-car garage, and above it is a full apartment—or at least there had been one—with bedroom, bathroom, kitchen, and living room, as spacious as the main house itself. My mother had lived in that apartment for a while.

But it's the garage I keep looking at. One of the garage doors is missing in the photo. In its place hangs a silver tarp.

"What the hell happened to the garage door?" I wonder to myself. To Katie, "What the hell am I going to do with this house? I don't know what kind of condition it's in. If there's drugs in there. Of all the things to inherit, I get a drug den. What am I supposed to do? Where do I even start?"

To which she says, "This is what lawyers are for."

Someone recommends Avvo to me. If you haven't heard of it, this is a website where you put in the type of lawyer you need (in this case probate) and the zip code of where you need it. I do a search and settle on a well-reviewed guy in the Nashville area.

I leave a message with his assistant and he calls me back the next day. I tell him my situation and he has questions. Don't we all.

"So it was your grandmother's house," he repeats. "But she died in March."

"Correct."

"And she had two children, your mother and your uncle, that were living in the house with her."

"That's right."

"But they didn't file the probate for the estate in the four months between your grandmother's death and your mother's."

"Is that strange?" I ask.

"Not unheard of," he tells me. "But it means we will have to file probate for both your mother and your grandmother in order to get the house transferred to you and Joe."

"Me *and* Joe?"

The lawyer proceeds to explain to me that when my grandmother died, if she didn't have a will, her estate would have been split 50/50 between her surviving children. Since my mother died, that means I get her half.

I would wonder later if Joe overlooked this detail. If

he'd hoped that with my mother out of the way, he would gain the house without contest.

"But his name isn't on the property," I tell him. "It's only my mother's name."

The idea of having to work with Joe, to collaborate with him for any reason at all—*no*.

"In that case, it means the house would be seventy-five percent yours and twenty-five percent his, because the home was jointly owned between your grandmother and mother, and he would've inherited half of your grandmother's half when she died. Either way, he still has claim, it's just a matter of how much claim."

"I don't want to work with him," I say, and know I must sound like a spoiled brat or one of those insane relatives I'm sure he's used to dealing with in probate situations. I try to temper it with a "You don't understand."

I explain about Joe being in jail. I explain that even if he wasn't, there would be no going over and talking to him. That he is violent, unpredictable. That he can't be trusted.

What the probate lawyer thinks of all this, I don't know. He probably dismisses me as a hysterical female, I'm sure, but the fact remains that there isn't a house in this world, no matter how grand, that I will walk into if Joe is there.

"You could always walk away," my wife tells me. My friends tell me the same. They say the ordeal—up to two years of talking to Joe, working with Joe—wouldn't be worth the minimal financial payoff.

One goes so far as to ask, "What is the price of your peace of mind?"

"Priceless," I tell her.

"Then let the damn house go."

And yet, I find myself digging in. I find myself thinking Joe doesn't deserve that house.

If he really killed my mother for money, for the property he stands to inherit—then *no*.

He *shouldn't* get to keep it. His plan should *completely* and totally *fail*.

This still leaves me with the matter of the looming mortgage. Now that I've made the mistake of calling the bank and telling them I stand to inherit the house, they have a new target.

Every two or three days I get a phone call. They ask me for an update. Press me for a payment, which I politely refuse.

What I need is to find out what's owed and what the payment is.

"I'm sure there's a bill in the mailbox," Katie suggests. "Or at least in the house."

"That means going *into* the house," I say. And a tremor runs through me. Excitement or fear, I can't be sure. "I don't know that I can do that."

"Why?" Katie asks. "It's *your* house."

I tell her about the videos on YouTube that show you how to wedge a screwdriver under a sliding glass door and pop it off its track. I imagine trying to do this in broad daylight without having a heart attack. I've never broken into anything before.

Okay, this is a lie. I broke into the public pool with some friends so I could skinny dip with this guy I had a crush on at the time. What can I say? At fifteen, I wasn't great at risk assessment.

But I'm an adult now. And I'm *very* aware that jail is a thing.

Katie is way ahead of me. She's already making a shared checklist in Trello. There are two lists, actually: first, what we want from the house—the mortgage documents, my grandmother's death certificate, important papers like my mom's health records, social security number, pictures and photos, and the necklace, if I can find it. She's also written down the self-addressed envelopes, because my mom had only written me back once but I'd sent five. That means there are four still in the house somewhere, and I'd rather Joe not have my address printed so plainly for him.

The second list is what we need to bring to the house to accomplish this search: gloves, masks, packing boxes, and a flathead screwdriver.

I've also got my birth certificate, my marriage license, and my driver's license on the list, so should the police show up and say—oh, well a neighbor called and said they saw a tall woman (Katie) heft a shorter woman (me) through a window and we are here to investigate the break-in—I can explain that while it is a break-in, it's not a *bad* one.

But surely there's an easier way to do this.

I call Detective Barnes and ask him if they'd locked the house when they took my uncle away. Best-case scenario, it's unlocked and I can just walk in. Unfortunately, Detective Barnes confirms that they locked up when they left. That the only set of keys to the house would be in the county lockup with Joe's possessions. I would have to ask Joe to give me the keys, and he would have to give me permission to have them.

Even if I was being eaten alive by zombies, I wouldn't ask Joe for a mercy kill—let alone his house keys.

Instead I explain what I found out about the house, what I'm trying to do with my mother's estate, to Detective Barnes.

"It sounds like a civil matter," he says to me, which I take as a polite way of telling me that he doesn't have time to deal with this. But then he surprises me by adding, "You may be able to get a locksmith to let you in if you show them your mother's death certificate and explain your situation."

A locksmith. A viable option.

After a few calls, I find one in the area who says that if I can show the certificate and my driver's license and paperwork proving I'm my mother's daughter, he'd be happy to let me into the house.

The idea of traveling during a pandemic isn't ideal, but it will give me a chance to pick up my mother's remains and find the mortgage information. To go through her personal effects and box up what I want to keep for myself.

"I don't know what we're going to find in there," I warn Katie. "It could be anything. Dirty needles between couch cushions. Drugs. Guns."

"I'm ready for anything," she replies, in true ride-or-die fashion.

Because my wife is working long hours now that her teaching job has moved online, Katie volunteers to go with me to the house. She assures me that regardless of whether or not we need a locksmith or a screwdriver, she's in.

I love her for it.

As I go through the motions of filling out probate paperwork, fielding calls with the lawyer, and manically refreshing Joe's court record, confirming again and again that his court date is still weeks away, that the charges against him haven't changed—I think a lot about my grandmother's house.

As a child I'd loved living in that house. Mostly because I loved my grandmother, but also because it was the most stable home I'd had thus far.

My grandparents had purchased that brick ranch house in the seventies and the interior was fascinating. The kitchen was wood paneling and yellow appliances, but the front room, sometimes called the sitting room or dining room, had Grecian statues and glass china cabinets and enough plants to give the impression of a forest.

My grandmother had an aloe plant that I loved in particular. It was so old, so grotesquely large, that it looked like something out of *Jurassic Park*.

The carpet was this thick gray-blue shag that I felt like I was sinking into whenever I walked on it. My bedroom was in the back, northeast corner, next to my grandparents'. I would later learn that it had also been my mother's childhood bedroom.

But when it was mine, it was overrun with stuffed animals and art supplies. Books of all kinds.

On most days, my grandmother would shove me outside in the morning and not call me in until lunch. I would play with the little girls down the street who had two Great Danes as big as horses, and when they got bored of running around their yard or I was sent away, I would spend the rest of the day climbing trees, rolling around in the dirt, following the creek bed that ran through the neighborhood.

Now that I think about it, no wonder I have an imagination. I was a lonely only child who literally played with trees and dirt for hours every day. That level of boredom must have conjured the need for a rich inner life.

One of my favorite non-dirt activities was to go with my grandmother down to the Salvation Army store—which smelled strangely of plastic and old lady perfume—and search the bins for new books, which she would buy as long as they were a quarter or less, and I could get up to four. That was my thrift store budget—one dollar. I could get as many as ten books with that if I was careful.

Arms full, I'd come home and flop onto my Rainbow

Brite bedsheets, shove away the mound of stuffed animals collected there, and spend the rest of the day reading.

My grandmother was tall with thick black hair and dark hazel eyes. I'd never known her to have a job, but as she sliced the skin off apples and salted the slices for me to eat, she would tell me stories about how she'd gone to cosmetology school when she was younger and had liked it. This was until my grandfather, in a jealous rage, had driven her car into the river with her cosmetology kit still inside. And that had been the end of her career as a stylist.

In place of this career, she became very active in her church, and had somehow become a pastor, often traveling around and giving sermons as a visiting preacher. Her favorite kind of church was the holy-rolling kind. The Pentecostals who would jump up and run through the aisles, forming a sort of frenzied congo line. This was unfortunate because I always had to go with her and I'm a bit lazy, so I didn't like running around in circles shaking my hands above my head.

But I had a plan for avoiding this.

There was always a moment early in the sermon where people could be healed. The pastor would call out, "Is there anyone here tonight that wants to be *touched* by the hand of God? Who wants to *feel* the Holy Spirit running through them?"

I would hop up from the pew immediately and get in line, sometimes feeling my grandmother make a desperate swipe for the big bow on the back of my dress, knowing full well what I was up to. But she couldn't try too hard or everyone would know she didn't want *me* to feel the Holy Spirit, so it was pretty easy to squirm past her.

"Oh, she's so enthusiastic! You must be so proud."

"I am," my grandmother would say with grim bitterness. "I really am."

Once I got to the front of the line, the pastor would call out, "Sweet Jesus! Will you move through this child tonight?"

"Yes, sir!" I would say because I thought I had to. Jesus wasn't here, so who else was going to answer this guy?

Then there'd be a bit of speaking in tongues on the pastor's part, and at the end, as if punctuating this performance, he'd strike me straight in the forehead. A clear, direct *bap*!

This was my cue.

I'd go stiff-legged and fall straight out on the red carpet. Demonstrating to my grandmother, and everyone else in the congregation, that I was so full of the Holy Spirit I'd been rendered unconscious.

Of course, I couldn't do this if my grandmother was preaching because she'd give me a stare so stern I'd be scared to close my eyes, let alone fall down and pretend to sleep.

But she didn't preach in her own church. So passing out was the perfect pardon from all that running around and speaking in tongues.

Instead, I could just take a nice nap and my grandmother would scoop me up off the floor at the end of the night, her bible under her arms, if she was feeling generous. If not, I'd get a rough toe in my ribs and a short "The Holy Spirit left. Get up."

My grandmother was there day in and day out in a way my mother hadn't been. By the late eighties, my mother's alcoholism was full blown.

No matter what was going on around me, Nana was there. Rolling oranges along the table before cutting a hole in the top for me to drink. Showing me how to make biscuits, forming the dough with an overturned water glass, flour dusted across my cheeks.

Asking me to brush her hair and joking that the mole on the back of her head was her third eye. "To keep a better eye on you."

More than that, she took me seriously. When I told her I couldn't sleep because the mouths in all the photographs in my room kept moving, she helped me to take them down. When I said that I couldn't fall asleep because there was a demon who stood in the doorway, a figure with red eyes that I called The Quaker Oat Man because of his wide-brimmed hat, she began to sleep with me.

She hid bright plastic eggs in the yard for me to find every Easter. Bought me new clothes for every holiday. Threw me birthday parties with big cakes. Ran my baths. Took me to school.

She had to be the one. When my father went to prison and my mother moved us back to Nashville to live with her parents, my mom started drinking and doing drugs in a way I'd never seen before. The drinking was nearly nonstop. She would disappear for days.

Once, when the officers came to my grandmother's house to arrest my mother for driving under the influence of liquor, I was outside, and so I had a front-row view of the spectacle.

It was the end of July.

I'd been running around the yard all day in the endless Tennessee heat, chasing dragonflies and the new dog—a Chow/German Shepherd mix—when I spotted the black-and-white patrol car rolling up the long driveway.

My mother had been standing on the patio, smoking, talking to my aunt, when they asked her name and called her over. She would've been twenty-six at the time.

As they began to cuff her, she resisted. She pushed one of them, adding an assault charge to the DUI.

Because she was drunk when this was happening, her

resistance increased in proportion to their efforts, until she devolved into something like a wildcat, screaming, hissing, and twisting in their arms.

At the sound of her scream, I bolted barefoot across the yard, trying to reach her. Her screaming, as it always did, caused a terrified, visceral reaction in me.

I had to reach her. I had to make sure she was okay.

I'd covered a lot of ground, making it all the way to the patio, before someone grabbed me.

I looked up. It was Nana who held me tight.

Nana, whose eyes were soft when she said, "No, baby. You stay with me."

I went slack in her grip, unable to do anything but watch the car back out of the driveway and take my mother away.

Then I was released.

Pulling grass from my hair, Nana told me not to worry, that my mother would be back.

She had to tell me this because I'd seen my father arrested, hauled away, and he hadn't come back. And she knew not knowing where my mother was made me restless, that putting me to bed that night would be nearly impossible.

But she would try. She would lie down beside me if she had to. And that mattered.

It wasn't always good between us—my grandmother and me. There were many years when she and I didn't talk, throughout my twenties, mostly, when I'd been angry—no, *furious*—that she kept taking Joe's side, kept excusing him, no matter what he did or who he hurt.

More than once Joe had beaten the hell out of her, leaving her face swollen shut, black and blue.

When asked why she put up with it, she replied simply, "He's my son."

And as admirable as loyalty may be, the ashtray incident was a deal-breaker for me. Her inaction almost cost my mother her life.

Yet in her final years, I'd softened.

I would ask to talk to her when I called my mom, catch up with her, find out how she was doing.

"I want to make it to eighty-five," she told me. "At least."

She said this four months before she died, when I called her on her birthday, just to tell her I loved her.

I'm glad I did.

The ghost in our attic was angry
we'd put planks over the window,
to keep the wood from rotting.

He woke the house when the wind
burst in, or maybe it wasn't a ghost…

—excerpt of the poem "The Looking Glass" from the chapbook *Evolution*

CHAPTER NINE

It's Friday July 24th, 2020, and I'm trying to pack for Tennessee. I'm looking at my list, trying to decide which suitcase I should take. Katie and I are texting back and forth. I'm telling her that Kim and I will arrive on Monday. That we can go to my grandmother's house on Tuesday and get whatever we need, whatever we find, and Kim can stay behind at Katie's place and work on her classes.

I wonder aloud what it will be like, walking through those doors after nineteen years of being away.

All of this is cut short when I get the notification on my phone. A simple text that says *Inmate Release Alert* with the day's date and time on it.

And my uncle's name.

The text is informing me that almost two weeks before his trial date, Joe has been set free.

I open Joe's arrest record and refresh it again as fast as my fingers allow.

My heart is pounding, my face hot.

The changed court date is the first thing I see. For

weeks it said August 5th. Now it reads today's date, the meeting time at nine this morning. Six hours ago.

I search the file updates, and the first case I find is the aggravated assault—strangulation—felony case. Its status reads:

Nolle prosequi without costs

My stomach sours.

The court abandoned my mother's strangulation case. They chose not to pursue it. Why?

How in the world could they just drop the charge?

Then I see the note.

Incarceration Special Conditions: victim is deceased

They dropped the case because my mother is dead.

Are you kidding me?

Their only reason for not hearing the case is because she's *dead*?

A whip-sharp headache cracks along the base of my skull.

How in the world did this case get dropped because "victim is deceased?"

It's not like she was the only witness.

I'm alive. I called the police that day. I have a phone record to prove it.

I could testify. The police who came to the house could testify, could relay what they wrote down, what they saw. Surely these details, the evidence, was recorded before a warrant was made.

Hell, or even the fact that he evaded arrest could be taken into account.

And why hadn't anyone come back to the house, tried to catch Joe by surprise in the seventeen months between the strangulation and her death that my mother *was* alive? Why, in fact, was her being alive even a requirement for the case to go forward?

I think of how the cops came to my grandmother's house in the summer of 1990 and arrested my mother for an outstanding DUI. They had no problem showing up to collect her. Why hadn't they done the same for Joe?

I don't know what I'd expected to feel if Joe was set free. I'd known all along that there was a strong possibility he wouldn't be charged with her death.

But now that he's free even for the strangulation, which I *know* he did, I am *so*...

Pissed.

Sure, there might be some lack of clarity about how responsible he was for her death, but the strangulation is no contest.

He did it.

There were witnesses, there was evidence.

How in the world does her *death* nullify that?

Are you telling me that if I shoot someone and they survive, then they are later killed by someone else before I go to trial, I'm good? Because they're already dead?

What?

"I don't understand," I lament to every person who will listen.

But I really shouldn't be surprised. This is the old pattern. Like the other 116 charges on Joe's record, which have nearly all been dismissed or reduced. Every time.

The two drug charges he incurred with this arrest are no different.

The other charge of which they had evidence, contraband in a penal institution—felony, was also nolle prosequi'd. They didn't even convict him of having the drugs in his body—the drugs they found. The meth and heroin he intentionally tried to bring into jail with him when he was arrested might as well have not existed at all.

As maddening as this is, it's the third charge that I find

most irritating. The misdemeanor charge, the possession or casual exchange charge, has the word *guilty* beside it.

Surprise. He was actually convicted of the misdemeanor, the most innocuous of the charges.

But what does it say beside *Incarceration Special Conditions*?

Time served.

Why bother convicting him at all if there are no consequences for what he's done?

This is the third time he has been convicted of a possession, casual exchange misdemeanor charge. In February of 2002, he got thirty days for his first possession misdemeanor, and in June of 2005 he got supervised probation for eleven months and twenty-nine days in lieu of any jail time for his second possession conviction.

And for this third charge, he only spent twenty nights in jail while waiting for the court date.

There's no mention of probation, or the fact that he's a repeat offender.

In an alternate universe, had he been convicted of the felony drug charge, of which they had evidence, and the felony strangulation, which he absolutely committed, that would've been his third felony. Tennessee has a third-strike law.

Three felonies and it's possible to spend life in prison without parole.

My mother's murder would have never had to see trial for justice to be served.

But that didn't happen.

Joe was set free. Every single time.

It's moments like this that illustrate why people are so disappointed in our justice system. How often it fails us. How often it should work, has every reason to work, and yet doesn't.

How the rage from that disappointment, of not being seen, heard, can build inside a person. How it can make them feel helpless. Beyond hurt.

I try to articulate those feelings to my wife and my friends.

How angry I am.

They listen, express their empathy, and despite the circumstances surrounding me, I find myself grateful again for all the loving, caring people who have come into my life in the last fifteen years.

All the people I have who love me—people my mother didn't have.

And just like that, my anger folds into sadness. Heartbreak for her. For everyone like her—unprotected, unheard.

"Even if he killed her," I tell Kim, "I'll never see justice. He's made of Teflon or something. None of these charges ever stick! Why?"

I wonder again if he's an informant, a narc for the Nashville drug department…or if I write too much crime fiction. Maybe somehow he really is that lucky.

Lucky enough to be arrested shortly after the jail had a coronavirus outbreak, and as the cases rose, they probably sought to empty their cells rather than fill them.

When I tell Katie I'm not coming to Tennessee on Monday as planned, that we can't possibly go to my grandmother's house because Joe will certainly be there, I feel a strange mixture of disappointment and relief.

I'd been nervous about going, the unease nipping at the back of my neck for weeks. I'd wondered if going to the house was a big mistake. If while cleaning I would've poked myself with one of his needles, or found something I could never unsee. I'd wondered if the cops had left my mother's room as they'd found it

—if seeing it like that would be more than I could bear.

And now I don't have to deal with any of that.

Katie tells me, "All I can think is that the universe is looking out for you."

"I hope so," I say. "You're probably right."

Katie also tells me not to give up. That the universe might surprise me. That situations like this are never resolved quickly and I just have to be patient.

"What are you going to do next?" she asks me.

I think about it. Then, that night, before closing my eyes to sleep, I reply: "Call him."

It's July 25th, 2020, at 3:58 p.m. when I call Joe. Almost twenty-four hours since I got the inmate release alert on my phone.

I pace my office, his number on my cell phone, my thumb hovering over the call button.

My heart is racing and my knees feel weak.

Either sit down or fall down, I think, and cross my office, out into our sunroom. I curl myself into the rattan chair, feeling the summer breeze ripple through the screens and tussle the long stems of the herbs I have growing in the boxes along the window's ledge.

I press call. Listen to the ring trill through the phone's speakers.

I focus on the heart-shaped leaves of the redbud tree swaying in the sunlight, try to draw enough air into my lungs to breathe.

After a minute of slow, melodic trills, I'm starting to think he won't answer.

Before I can figure out if I'm relieved or disappointed, he picks up. "Hello?"

"Hi. It's me, Kory."

"You were on my list of people to call," he says.

I register the strained condition of his voice. It's high, strident. Not unlike my mother's voice when she straddled the line between uncontrollable laughter and tears.

I don't know if he's distressed and it's adrenaline or panic I hear, or if he's high on something. Regardless of the cause, it's clear he isn't entirely in control of himself.

I proceed with caution.

"Why were you arrested?" I ask. I don't mention the strangulation charge or warrant. I don't reveal that the police called me, asked me questions about his history of violence against my mother.

"Because I opened my big mouth," Joe says. "The cops were all here, and one of them said, 'Just another dead junkie,' and I lost it, Kory. I *lost* it."

He sounds like he's about to lose it now.

"No one's going to talk about my sister that way. *No one.*"

"So they arrested you for fighting a cop?"

"I knew I was going to get my ass kicked, I just didn't know how many it was going to take. Four of 'em, apparently. They knocked out one of my teeth, but I got in a good blow or two myself. But they had to let me go. They couldn't keep me on any of that."

"Why not?" I ask.

"Because my lawyer got them to release their body cams. It showed the whole thing. Showed them beating up on me and what they said. One even told me no one should've talked about my sister like that, and I thanked him for it, I did."

"They dropped all the charges," I say.

This is the first time I hear this story. Detective Barnes

made no mention of a fight, or my uncle resisting. And there was no resisting arrest charge added to the record.

So I don't know what, if any, of this is true.

And it's important to remember that this man lies like he breathes. Once, he stole the stove and refrigerator from a firefighter's driveway while the home was being refurbished. The firefighter had come home from work and found his appliances missing. The police went to the nearby recycling facility, found the appliances, and my uncle's face on the surveillance footage. Joe was arrested and held on a $15,000 bond.

The lies he'd told to the facility attendants in order to sell the appliances for scrap, and the lies he'd told the police to avoid arrest, the lies he's probably telling me now—

How much practice he must have.

I tell Katie about the stolen appliances, but admit I can't remember when it happened. It takes her no time at all to find the 2015 news article in *The Tennessean*.

"I just got home," he says. "Kory, if you could see the place right now, you'd be in tears. It's torn up to hell and back."

"Why would they tear up the house?"

"They thought I'd killed her!" he cries out. "They were looking for a murder weapon or something, I guess. But this place is an absolute wreck. Just demolished."

"Why would they think you killed her? You said you thought she'd died of an overdose." I reopen the old argument to see what version of the story will emerge now.

"I do think that," he says. "I know what an overdose looks like, and she was blue just like that."

He's sticking to the original script, his words unchanged.

"But how could she have gotten ahold of anything? You said you had everything locked up?"

His exasperation grows. "Damn it, I don't know. I came home and my safe was busted open in the middle of the concrete patio. I don't know if the police did that or she did."

Here we have our first variation in the story. He would've absolutely seen his safe dashed on the patio long before the police had come. My mother slept at one end of the house, he slept at the other.

Between the two, he would've had to walk right past the sliding glass doors, and would've had a full view of the patio. Not to mention, the safe was in his bedroom.

As if he wouldn't have noticed it missing, and being the addict he was, wondered where the hell his drugs had gone, not to mention the impossibility of my weak, sick mother picking up a safe and carrying it anywhere. A medium fireproof safe weighs at least a hundred pounds.

In order for this new version of the story to be true, three unlikely things would have had to happen:

Before entering my mother's bedroom and finding her dead, he would've had to wake up in his room and exit it without noticing his safe was missing. Unlikely.

Secondly, he would've had to walk in front of the glass doors and not see a busted safe with his drugs all over the patio (also unlikely). He would've had to continue to not see it or check his safe after finding her, after calling the police, after spending hours in the house waiting for them to arrive. After letting the dogs out. After searching my mom's room.

Lastly, the meth and heroin he'd had in his body when he was arrested would have to have been in his body for... what, a whole day?

Because if he kept his drugs in there, when did he

remove the heroin and meth so he could hide it in his body?

All of this is overlooking the glaring impossibility that my mother, with her chronic health problems, would've had the strength to dash a safe against the concrete long enough to crack it open and get to the drugs.

At this point, I simply don't believe the story about the safe.

If he really had come home in the middle of night and found her collapsed on the floor, as was told in one version of the tale, maybe he wouldn't have been able to see the patio if it was dark outside.

But wouldn't he have checked his safe at least once all through the night and into the morning, before the police came?

Yet maybe he's telling the truth. Maybe now, as we talk, his safe is dashed open on the patio, its contents spread wide in the hot July sun. If so, the vandalism would've happened after my mother died. If the police had to crack open the safe—it means the safe was locked tight when they arrived.

And my mom never broke into it. She didn't steal drugs from him.

"I was in there for twenty-one nights," he tells me.

"It must've been hard," I say. I mean this. To go cold turkey when struggling with an addiction can't be easy.

It must've been hell.

"Oh, it was nothing," he says.

"Really? I thought you were still addicted to heroin," I say.

"No, I was down to taking almost nothing. I'd almost weaned myself completely."

He makes no mention of the new drug charges, nor the

fact he was found guilty of a misdemeanor possession charge.

I find it hard to believe that he would be motivated enough to hide meth and heroin inside himself if he was "almost weaned." Again, I realize he has no idea that I've been following him so closely.

Since he hasn't brought up the charges, I don't press him.

"I took care of Mom," I tell him.

"Good, good," he says. He has something in his mouth. The chewing is as manic as his words. "When I'd called down there and they told me she was still in the freezer, that'd pissed me off."

He does sound pissed, though with concern for my mom or for another reason, I can't tell. Is he angry that his evidence is still lying around?

"There was a delay with the paperwork, but it's done. They're just waiting for the funeral home to pick her up. They told me it might take a minute."

"Yes, ma'am. It took me ten days to get my momma back."

God, I wish he'd stop eating.

"Do you want some of them?" he asks.

"What?" I ask, confused by the question.

"I mean, not to be morbid, but I could send you some of them."

"Them," it turns out, is ashes from the family urn. He describes it like he has generations of family members in a single urn. But I do a quick calculation and realize he must mean my aunt and grandmother. My grandfather was buried in an unmarked grave in Mount Olivet Cemetery.

"I had to dump some of them out to get the rest in," he tells me.

The idea of him collecting all of the family in a single

urn disturbs me. I do not offer to send him some of my mother.

"Kory, listen. Things between your mom and I weren't perfect, but we loved each other."

Quite a reversal, I think, from the "Your mother didn't love anyone, but she loved you" line he fed me on the morning she'd died.

"Like the time she hit me with the glass ashtray—that wasn't fun!"

Hit him with the glass ashtray? Is he delusional?

Or does he really think I've forgotten what happened? That my memory could simply be rewritten if he told me enough lies. That he could confuse and manipulate me into trusting him.

As if the medical examiner wouldn't ask me what the hardware in her skull had been for.

"If you come down here to get your momma, come by and see me," Joe says. "Even if you yell at me from the end of the drive, I'd love to see you."

What a slap in my mother's face it would be if I saw Joe. I'd used his presence in her life, in that house, as an excuse for why I wouldn't visit her or my grandmother for years.

I couldn't forgive myself if I visited him once she was gone.

In this emotional whirlwind of a conversation, I've almost forgotten why I called.

"Joe, we need to talk about the house."

"What about the house?" he asks.

"What do you want to do with it?" I ask.

"Sell it," he says without pause. "There's too many bad memories in this place."

Good, I think. We might have common ground. If he

wants to sell it, great. We can do that, split the money, and move on with our lives.

"Well, first we need to sort the mortgage. The mortgage company keeps calling me, asking me for a payment, but they won't tell me how much it's for."

"They shouldn't be doing that. I'll call them and tell them to stop."

"But the mortgage——" I begin.

"Don't worry about it," he says. "I'm about to handle it."

"With what money?" I ask. Drug money?

Or a pending life insurance policy?

"That's irrelevant," he says. "I'll have that paid off here in a few days."

"Joe, my mother's name is on this house, which means now it's half mine. I don't want the house and you want to sell it, so let's just do that." I hope to make it clear that I just want to resolve this as peacefully and quickly as possible.

There's a long pause, and then he abruptly says, "Right. Okay, well, I'd prepared for this. I'll have the lawyers get in touch with you, show you a copy of the will and all that. I hate that it has to be like this, but it is what it is."

And he ends the conversation.

The call lasted twenty-seven minutes.

SOMETIMES I FORGET THAT MY UNCLE WAS ONLY FIFTEEN when I was born. That when he was living at Nana's with us during my childhood, he would've been in his early twenties.

What I remember most clearly from those days were his love of aviator sunglasses and his resemblance to Jim

Morrison. He had the same thick curly brown hair, and my uncle played a wild rift on the guitar.

"I was really into it," my aunt Lana would tell me later, as she described how she met and married Joe before birthing him two kids. "The rock and roll bad boy vibe was sexy as hell."

I admit I didn't see it. I remember my uncle standing shirtless on the side of the house, a little drunk and pissing against the brick facade with a cigarette hanging out of his mouth, the gold chain around his neck catching the light.

Of course, it was thirty years ago, when I lived in my grandmother's house, and it's been twenty years since my grandfather's funeral.

To update my memory, I search Facebook for a photograph and find one from 2013. His hair is still curly, but even longer, trailing past his shoulders in wiry ringlets. His eyes are still dark brown like my grandfather's. A sparse goatee and mustache surround his mouth.

The acne pockmarks on his face haven't lessened with time. And he's still tall. Still lean.

But there is a deep sadness to his eyes that I don't remember. Joe from long ago had fire in his eyes. An anger that was palpable even when contained beneath the surface of his skin, his words.

I don't see the anger now. In this photo, he looks like a man haunted.

My resolve wavers. My mind tries to reconcile the possibility that this man who has caused so much pain is also a deeply wounded man. It's not a comfortable position to occupy.

It isn't like I can just forget what he's done.

You might be wondering if my uncle ever put his hands on me or if my mother was his only target.

No, she wasn't. He's put his hands on my mother, his

mother, and the women he's dated. He's put his hands on his kids. I was told later that he'd broken his oldest son's collarbone by slamming him against the wall when he was twelve or thirteen. Someone else said it had been the boy's arm, not his collarbone. Joe broke something, whatever it was.

And yes, he put his hands on me. Once, when I was seventeen.

It was when I'd driven to Nashville for my grandfather's funeral in March 2001.

When I arrived, I found a house I didn't recognize.

Things were much worse than when I'd lived there as a child. My aunt Renee, who I'd only known to ever smoke weed and have a beer, was smoking a crack pipe in the bathroom.

My uncle was yelling at everyone, opening and slamming cabinets. Shoving people—me included—out of his way.

I'd known that my grandfather had been the strong arm of the family. That he'd kept everyone in line with his will alone.

I just hadn't realized how quickly things would devolve without his control.

I wonder if it began before his slow, painful death of emphysema. Probably as soon as he was too sick, too breathless to put up a fight.

When I found my aunt Renee smoking crack in the bathroom on the day of my grandfather's funeral and told her that I thought she shouldn't be doing this in front of children—Joe's kids were both under ten at the time—Joe came to her defense. He called me a "fucking dyke" who needed to mind her mouth before he minded it for me.

I responded with a similar expletive and he reacted.

He tried to wrap his hands around my throat, but I

blocked this attempt, barely, breaking the sunglasses I was wearing. It left an angry scratch on my nose, but this was hardly the worst casualty possible.

I followed with a hard shove that toppled him just long enough to give me a chance to run out of the house before he could right himself.

I made it through the neighbor's back door about four seconds before he did.

He was arrested soon after. I watched through the neighbor's window as he was shoved into the back of the police car, cuffed. I was told it was Nana who'd called the police.

Of course, as I've said, it isn't like he stayed in jail.

"Didn't you say there was a rumor Joe poisoned your grandfather and that's why he died?" Katie asks.

"That's what his wife, Lana, had said, that Joe had 'helped him along' with rat poison or something."

"If he's found guilty of murdering your mom, maybe they'll exhume his body and find out he killed him too. Then you'll be related to an actual serial killer."

I think of my grandfather's unmarked grave. Of the fact that even though each of them, my grandmother, my uncle, and my mother, received money when he died, none of them bothered to purchase a headstone for the man.

Soon I would find out why.

Dandelion seed, blowing.
White fluff,
floating above cracked pavement,
wilting tulip beds…

How much desire
is tossed about in the world?

How rarely
it anchors, sprouts, blooms.

—excerpt of the poem "spring melancholy" from the collection *Then Came Love*

CHAPTER TEN

I call my lawyer that afternoon and tell him that Joe made mention of a will. That he should reach out to Joe's lawyer and see if a will for my grandmother does, in fact, exist.

Kim, Katie, and I all expect this to be just another lie. Another ploy to buy time or form another scheme. And I hate the idea that he is going to make this difficult. That if he resists, probate is definitely going to stretch on for years.

Imagine my surprise when I get a call from my lawyer the next day, and in a sympathetic voice, he says, "I'm sorry, but I have some bad news."

The first piece of bad news is the discovery of a quitclaim deed from 2005, in which my mother signed away her rights to the house.

Combing back through the public record documents, I'm able to paint a clearer picture of the house's history. It was purchased by my grandparents in July of 1971. When my grandfather died without a will in March of 2001, ownership of the house was split—half for my grandmother and half for his two living children, giving a quarter claim each to my mother and Joe. My aunt Renee, being a step-child and my grandmother's first-born, received nothing.

At this time, the house had been paid for in full.

My mother's claim was terminated in July 2005, when she signed the quitclaim deed and relinquished her ownership to my grandmother.

Then Joe's quitclaim came in April 2008, just two days after he'd appeared in court and been found guilty of criminal trespassing. His signature conveyed to my grandmother full and complete ownership of the house. No doubt this was a financial decision. Because that year, she took out a $12,000 loan from the mortgage company I'd heard so much from lately. The dates on the loan application the lawyer sends confirm this.

Since that was twelve years ago, this means whatever is outstanding on the mortgage can't be much. Three thousand maybe, when considering they'd also been paying the property taxes from the mortgage payment.

Joe's credit or arrest record probably made this transfer from him to my grandmother a necessity. She would've had better credit and no arrest record of any kind. Regardless, it meant that upon my grandmother's death, her one hundred percent ownership of the house should've been split between her two surviving children. Fifty/fifty ownership between Joe and my mother.

In theory.

The second piece of bad news—the killing blow—arrives in my inbox soon after.

The email from my lawyer has a single attachment. I open it on my computer:

Last Will and Testament. Then my grandmother's name.

I, a resident of Nashville, Tennessee, being of sound mind and disposing memory, do hereby make this my last will and testament and do hereby revoke all other wills made and codicils by me.

I do hereby appoint my son as the executor of my estate to serve without bond, and I do hereby waive the filings of any accountings and inventory by him.

I do hereby give, devise, and bequeath all my property of which I die to be seized by my son, absolutely and in fee simple.

The will is punctuated with my grandmother's signature and dated December 30th, 2008.

"Is this a binding will?" I ask my attorney.

"It appears so," he says.

"She left him everything," I say in disbelief. "She completely wrote my mother out of the will."

"Do you know any reason why your grandmother would do that?" he asks.

"No," I say coldly. "I have no idea why she would do that."

At the time it may have been a financial decision, but that doesn't tell me why she'd leave my mother with nothing. Why she wouldn't at least give back what was already hers.

Unless she really believed that Joe would look after her, take care of her—make sure she got what she deserved.

"Well. Did your mother have anything else?"

Only me, I think.

And remember how my mother would cup my face in her hands, kiss my nose, my forehead, and cheeks until I was laughing. Over the laughter she'd say, "You're the most precious thing in my life. I wouldn't trade you for all the money in the world."

"No," I tell him, the old sadness rolling through me again. "She didn't have anything else."

The lawyer goes on to explain that since our business is done, he won't need to take the case to court for me, and he'll return what's left of my retainer by mail. I thank him and hang up.

My feelings remain mixed in the weeks that follow.

On the one hand, I'm deeply relieved.

There will be no battle. No years of having to work with Joe, possibly appearing in court beside him, making arguments or defending my mother's rights. I would've done it, of course.

I have no problem taking up arms when necessary, but it wouldn't have been fun.

It would've been exhausting and emotionally draining at the very least. Economically perilous at its worse.

But here I'm given the perfect excuse to bow out, to step away from all the madness and salvage my own sanity and peace of mind.

If only the relief would last.

Too quickly it vacillates with irritation and anger on my mother's behalf. I hate that the people she loved, relied on, had manipulated her—whether my mother realized it or not.

And who did the manipulation? My grandmother? Joe?

Because Joe didn't *quit* anything in 2005. He held on to his claim for three more years, until my grandmother needed to finance the $12,000 loan for the back taxes on the property.

But it's more than that.

Did they really care so little for her well-being? About what was fair? Or had my grandmother believed, perhaps rightfully, that my mother would always need care—and for some reason I'll never understand had actually trusted Joe to provide that care?

Joe had once said to me, "I promised our parents that

as long as she was alive, my sister would always have a place here. I'd always look after her."

As long as *she* was alive...maybe it was never about money. Maybe it was about promises.

Joe believes himself to be a man of his word. A loyal family man. Knowing that he needed to sell the house and move on, perhaps he felt he needed to be rid of my mother first in order to do that. That he was simply taking care of business, keeping his promises.

Or at least, that's what he told himself.

That evening I call Shay, my mother's ex, and give her the update on the probate situation. I've been checking in with her more and more in the weeks since my mother died.

First, because it's nice to talk to someone who knows my mom, who understands her as well as I did. We share all the same frustrations about my mom's choices to return to her childhood home again and again, placing herself in Joe's reach each time.

Shay is dealing with many of the same emotions I am: guilt, regret.

"I should've had her come here and stay with me. I've got an extra bedroom," she says. "When I called, I'd told her about Momma and Henry dying. Then she didn't remember the next time. I should've known then somethin' wasn't right."

This is our third or fourth conversation.

I'd reached out through Facebook first, knowing that she would want to know my mom had passed, being as she was the last real friend my mother had. No one, except for me, had talked to her in years.

When Shay got back to me, I told her the news, what the police had said.

She wasn't surprised.

"How many times have we told her he was gonna kill her? How many damn times, Kory?"

I can't argue. Though admittedly, I'd expected a violent death.

Apparently, so had Shay. Because when I tell her there is no real physical damage to my mom's body, that Joe claims it was an overdose, she refuses to believe it.

"No damn way," she says. "She liked her pills, true enough. That damn doctor in Tullahoma just kept givin' them to her. Somas, valium. It didn't matter. Made me so mad they don't ever punish those doctors for what they do. But there ain't a pill she liked that'd kill her! And she ain't fool enough to take a whole damn bottle!"

It's not only the doctors that are to blame, I think.

I was fourteen or fifteen when I got a skin graft in my mouth. The surgeon cut a piece of skin from the roof of my mouth and sewed it along the bottom of my teeth. They did this to repair gum loss and in preparation for the braces I would never have.

When I woke up with a sore mouth, to stitches and gauze I couldn't stop tonguing to save my life, they'd given me a prescription for pain pills.

I took one that night, when the pain was the worst.

I got through half a bowl of cereal before I was drooling on myself, staring into the chocolate puffs as if I was going to divine my future in the milk.

Shay, laughing, took the bowl away.

"I think that's enough for now," she said. "Give it up before you fall in it."

Because I hadn't liked how the pills had made me feel,

like my body was heavy and uncontrollable, like something I didn't own, I didn't want to take any more.

When my mom asked if she could have what was left, I didn't put up a fight.

If she took them immediately or added them to her collection, I don't know.

I think of the row of kitchen cabinets in the home my mother and I shared with Shay for almost ten years (not including the back-and-forth shuffling between my mom and dad, common for kids with divorced parents).

In the early nineties, I could open three cabinets and see the pill bottles stretching from one side of the door to the other.

They stood in little rows, orange bottles with their white caps filling *both* shelves, top and bottom—several rows deep.

I have more than a few memories of her pulling a bottle down after she got home from work. Of her standing at the bathroom sink, cupping her hand under a running faucet and gathering just enough water to throw the pill back.

"He's not saying it's pills," I tell her. "He's saying it's heroin."

"A bunch of horseshit."

"What if it was a pill that killed her?" I ask. "I hear they're mixing all kinds of crazy things into pills these days."

Whereas I can't so much as take my vitamins and probiotics without choking on my own tongue.

"If there was a pill, how the hell'd she get it?" Shay asks. "And don't tell me that bullshit about the broken safe. You know she couldn't have managed that. He must think we're dumb as hell."

How'd she get ahold of a pill?

It's a good question. If Joe is the sort of man to keep his drugs locked in a safe, I can't imagine a viable scenario in which he dropped a pill or left one in the sink.

That somehow in between setting pans on fire on the stove or stuffing things in the freezer, my mom had managed to find a pill between the couch cushions.

And if there had been one sitting on the bathroom sink? Would he have left it there on purpose? Hoping, *knowing*, she couldn't resist?

That all his talk about locking up her medicine to keep her safe might be just another lie—a manipulation to divert our attention from the truth.

Talking to Shay makes me miss my mom. Her voice. Shay's got that sweet southern lilt too. To ease the ache, I ask Shay, "How did you and Mom meet?"

If I can have nothing, I'll take a story. A reminder that my mother had been here and alive, once upon a time.

Shay laughs, the warmth in her voice deepening. I've always loved this about Shay. The word *good-natured* has never fit anyone so well.

"We met at The Cabaret. It was a gay bar in Nashville. Your mom was putting makeup on the drag queens."

"That night?" I ask.

"For a while, I think. She'd do it before they went on stage for their shows."

"So she came over and said hi, or what?"

"Sort of. She pulled my friend's hair."

I laugh. "*What?*"

"We had tails back then." Before she goes on, I'm already picturing the mullets. "And she came up and pulled my friend's. When she turned around, your momma apologized, saying that she'd thought my friend was someone else, someone she knew."

Likely story, I think.

"I asked her to join us. We got to talking, and turns out we did know some of the same people. I'd known your aunt Renee for ten years already, but hadn't crossed paths with your momma. I went home with her that night. Kory, I hadn't *never* done something like that—a one-night stand. And I'd only been broken up with Linda for a month. I wasn't even lookin' for nobody."

"How did we end up moving in with you?"

"Well, your momma got into it with that roommate of hers. She'd beat her up pretty good, actually. And she called me to come and get her. So I did. She looked like hell, with all those bruises. You know your momma bruised easy."

"She did."

"That weekend I moved you both out here to my trailer in Manchester. This was ninety-one, I believe. It wasn't always good times, but sometimes we were happy. Real happy."

"Yeah." I hold the phone a little tighter. "We were."

I DON'T REMEMBER THE EXACT MOMENT WE MOVED TO Shay's trailer in Manchester, Tennessee, but I do remember being happy there. It was a clean, well-lit place. Two bedrooms—one for my mom and Shay and one for me.

I even had my own bathroom.

Shay had bought me a brand-new day bed. A dresser for my clothes.

It was quieter than my grandmother's, which I liked, and because both Mom and Shay had to work during the day, I was a latchkey kid.

Usually I was dropped off at school in the morning on their way to work and I walked myself home.

It was an easy route, less than a mile, and entirely through quiet, safe neighborhoods.

Back then the street before mine had a little market called Mrs. Carter's Grocery—nothing more than a one-room shack with rough wood walls, a couple of aisles, and some cold cases full of drinks and ice cream. I would pop in on my walk home and buy candy or ice cream with the change my mom had left on the counter that morning.

Then the rest of the evenings were entirely my own.

Sometimes I read or watched television. Other times I went exploring.

I was free to come and go as I pleased as long as I was home by dark, and I always left a note.

Close to the house was a park called Old Stone Fort. This archeological park could be accessed by ducking behind any of the houses at the edge of my neighborhood.

Turns out that the stone structure for which the park was named was built thousands of years ago by the prehistoric natives from the area. Of course, I didn't know any of this at the time.

I just knew that it was a dense forest, wilder than anything I'd ever known.

It was what you might imagine if someone said "the woods," as in, "As I child, I loved to play in the woods."

There were winding riverbeds and trees so tall I couldn't see the tops of them. Sometimes I saw snakes or turtles or frogs. Birds of all kinds. Deer, rabbits.

Apart from tormenting the wildlife, I loved playing in the water.

In some places it was deeper than I was tall.

In other places, it was little more than a creek bed. When I was much older, my friends and I would jump off the cliffs—the place had more waterfalls than I could count —and swim in the blue waters below.

These streams were offshoots of the Little Duck River, and perfect for swimming and splashing. The water's edge was often trimmed by wide, warm stones on which to dry myself in the sun before starting the walk home.

Comparatively, this wilderness made the tiny creek that ran behind the houses in my grandmother's neighborhood look like a puddle. So it was easy to lose myself for hours investigating the underside of rocks, climbing branches for a better view of the forest around me, or running across fields with grass so high it came up to my chest.

Once, after a particularly hard rain, my friends and I went into the woods only to find it saturated. By the time I made it home, I was covered from head to toe in mud. When I knocked on the back door, standing on the deck rather self-consciously, I had to beg Shay to let me in.

Her jaw dropped when she saw me. Then she burst into laughter.

"My god, where have you been? *Look at you.* It's like you've been tarred!"

She only agreed to let me in after she'd hosed me down —literally—with the pipe hanging from a hook on the back deck.

Another time, when I arrived home from school with hours of freedom stretching out before me, I decided I wanted to take a bubble bath.

The private bath attached to their room had a jacuzzi tub, with the jets that would sputter as long as the dial on the wall was running. Once the timer ran out, it would automatically turn off.

I liked bubble baths. So when I ran the bath, I added Mr. Bubble's syrupy pink liquid to the gushing water.

I must've been very tired, because I fell asleep to the low ticking of the timer, the warm jets pounding my little limbs.

When I woke up, there were bubbles all right.

Everywhere.

They'd overflowed from the tub and onto the bathroom floor. Then they'd kept going.

As I leaned out of the tub, peering into the bedroom, I saw that the bubbles had spread all the way through and out into the kitchen.

"Oh no. Ohhhh. *Nooooo.*"

My nine-year-old body clambered wet and naked out of the tub, desperately trying to get the timer on the wall to stop fueling the traitorous jets. Once it did, I grabbed a towel and tried to soak up the bubbles.

This was useless. Two or three swipes soaked a towel and left me with a mountain of bubbles to contend with.

I was still naked, covered in bubbles, when Shay and Mom came home from work. They found me in the kitchen with a broom as I was trying to sweep the bubbles outside onto the deck.

When they saw me, my lip quivered. Tears filled my eyes. I thought I was going to be in so much trouble for using the tub without permission.

But instead, once they recovered from the shock of seeing half their house filled with bubbles, they laughed.

They laughed so hard they were the ones crying.

ONE OF MY FAVORITE MEMORIES, AS SIMPLE AS IT SOUNDS, IS Sunday mornings. As I would sit at the breakfast table, trying to wake up, Shay would look at me, smile, and say, "Let's go!"

I'd race her to the green Mustang and ride shotgun as the two of us went down to the Spring Street Market, a small grocery store up the road from us.

There, she'd buy the Sunday paper, a fat, unwieldy thing that came with a comics section.

She'd hand the comics over dutifully and I'd read them at the kitchen table while eating my Sunday morning pancakes. I think I love this memory so much because it shows how steady, how calm, this period of my life was. That I finally had things I looked forward to, that I enjoyed. I felt safe, mostly.

I felt loved.

And I think my mother had been happy too. That these were her good years.

All my memories of her smiling, of her enjoying herself, are from the years we lived with Shay. I'd never heard her laugh before—in a way that wasn't forced, showy. Never known her to spend so many days at a time in a manageable routine.

Of course, it wasn't always good.

There was the incident where she forgot to come to my performance. There were the evenings when she would come home from work, bone tired and irritable, and start drinking even before dinner. On some of those nights I'd wake to Shay yelling, and run from my bedroom to theirs, expecting the worst, only to find my mother in their closet, pissing into the dirty clothes basket because she was too drunk to find the bathroom.

Or on the nights when, after a hard day at her factory job, she'd call me into her room and ask me to pop and squeeze the blisters on her fingers while issuing grave warnings like "Stay in school, Kory. Work with your brain, not your body."

Or pointing at her grayed teeth and explaining, "The lithium did this. They put me on it when I was just a kid and it messed up my teeth. You want your teeth to look like this? You better brush them!"

There were also the moments when my mom would cheat on Shay, either leaving with a random person from the bar they'd gone to together or sneaking around with someone at work.

When this happened, they'd fight. Once, Shay packed all of my mother's things into the green Mustang and threw them into some guy's yard.

They always got back together, smoothed things over.

Even with more good times than I'd ever seen before, we couldn't fully escape my mother's sadness.

It could be felt like a thick, consuming mist that dampened everything.

One day when I was fourteen or fifteen, I came home from school and found that my mother and Shay were already home. They were on the back deck with their friends, drinking, grilling. Talking over each other and the music blaring from the stereo.

My mother was morose, tears openly spilling from her eyes.

That's when I remembered that her court date had been that day.

I could tell by her face alone, by the way she tipped the bottle back, that she'd gotten bad news. She'd been convicted with her third or fourth DUI. She'd been sentenced to 120 days in jail.

Yet everyone was trying to cheer her up. Make her smile.

"Come on, Leitha. Four months is nothing! It'll pass by in no time!"

"Yeah, they could've been so much stricter with you, hon! You got lucky!"

But when my mother threw the beer bottle back again and took another deep drink, she didn't look lucky at all.

That night, when Shay popped her head into my

bedroom to tell me goodnight, I quietly asked, "What's going to happen to me?"

She frowned, coming into the room and closing the door behind her. "What do you mean, hon?"

"When Mom goes to jail. Where—What am I going to do?"

Her face softened as she sank onto the foot of my bed. "You'll be here with me, if you want to be."

The relief of not being sent away was almost enough to soften the blow of a Thanksgiving and Christmas without my mother.

While the other kids at school chatted excitedly about the family they'd see, the food they'd eat, the trips they'd take, I was in store for a very different experience.

On Thanksgiving morning, before we ate, Shay and I drove down to the Coffee County Jail. We were patted down, checked over, then escorted to the visitors' area.

"You first, hon," Shay said, after we were informed that only one person could see her at a time. "She'll be glad to see you."

But my mother didn't look glad as I settled down onto the wobbly metal stool on my side of the plexiglass. She looked worn and sad, the circles under her eyes pronounced, her blonde hair dark at its roots.

She looked embarrassed.

She lifted the plastic phone from its receiver, and I did the same.

"Well, here we are," she began, forcing a smile and the practiced vivaciousness which I understood even then was a mask for the pain beneath. "Tell me what delicious things you ate today. The food here is terrible."

"I haven't eaten yet," I tell her. "But Shay got a small turkey and a box of those mashed potatoes we like. And a pie."

My mom smacked her lips, following through with her show of good cheer.

"Enjoy yourself, baby," she said. "For both of us."

I run through these memories with Shay, sharing the laughs. She tells me she has a photograph of me as a teenager. She was on the riding lawn mower, in the middle of cutting the yard, and I'd stopped her, leaning over the wheel with the most ornery face.

"You were gettin' onto me about somethin'," she says.

"Sorry," I say. "I'm sure I was an asshole as a teenager."

"No, hon. You were a good kid. Always reading. And I guess it paid off, didn't it? Look at you. An *author*."

She says this as if it's a far more glamourous job than it is. As if I don't spend my days in my pajamas, snacking excessively, often consumed by existential dread.

"I just don't understand why Nana would cut Mom out of the will. Why would she do that? Why does she keep throwing her own daughter to the wolves?"

"She's always been like that, ever since Leitha was a kid, after what Hank did."

Hank. When she says this, I assume she means my mother's half-brother, my grandfather's oldest son from a previous marriage. Hank, the brother who'd climbed into her bed at night and molested her.

"She didn't believe her about what her brother did?" I ask, wondering if now, at long last, I'm going to get the full story of what happened.

"Not Hank Jr.," Shay corrects me. "*Hank Sr.* Your granddad."

"Papaw?" I ask, alarm spreading through me. "What did Papaw do to her?"

There's a pause, and through the window I watch a cat jump out of the bushes and pounce. But the cardinal flies away unharmed.

Finally, Shay says, "I don't know if you need to hear this, hon."

As if I'd give up so easily. "Tell me."

I don't ask her why, I know—there is a shade,
paler than white and the whole world wears it sometimes.

—excerpt of the poem "despondent as Edna Pontellier"
from the chapbook *Evolution*

CHAPTER ELEVEN

How well do you know your mother? Truly? If you were adopted, orphaned, or otherwise separated from her, you're excused from this interrogation. But for the rest of us, how well do you know her? Think about it.

Rarely do we ask our mothers about their lives before us. Rarely do we glean more than the details shared in passing. Usually little to nothing from their childhoods, as we're too busy living our own.

In my case, this is the version of my mother's life that I'd heard before her death:

She'd grown up in Nashville, Tennessee, with my grandparents. She was one of four kids in the house, though she was the first born to my grandfather and grandmother. Hank Jr. was my grandfather's first child from his first marriage. My aunt Renee was my grandmother's first child from *her* first marriage. My mom and Joe were two children they had together, Joe being the youngest by five years.

I'd been told that by twelve my mother had tried to kill

herself. That around the same time she'd developed seizures. That she'd never finished eighth grade.

That her peak horror experience had been when my mother's grandmother, Mamie, had cooked my mom's pet rabbit and served it to her for dinner.

That my mother had run away at sixteen with David #1.

That by eighteen, she'd left David #1 and had begun traveling around the church circuit with my grandmother.

My grandmother preached. My mother sang.

It was in a church not far from St. Louis, MO, that she met my father, June 1982, two months before she turned nineteen. Within three months, she'd married him, and she stayed with him until he was convicted of rape in 1988.

I'd also heard that Hank Jr., the older half-brother, had molested her. That sometimes at night, he'd climb into her bed, touch her. But the few times this had been mentioned, I'd been under the impression that it hadn't happened often and had been quickly ended.

I'd never put it together that the attempted suicide had been the result of sexual assault. That her addiction problems were caused by PTSD and chronic, severe, unresolved trauma—

Until I hear the *revised* version of my mother's life. The one no one was brave enough to tell me until after she'd died.

What Shay tells me, what comes after "Your grandfather was the worst" and "I don't know if you need to hear this, hon," pulls my mother's entire life into clear, unwavering focus.

It's like putting on glasses for the first time and realizing just how out of focus the picture had been all along.

"Tell me," I insist, adjusting the phone in my hand. "I'm just going to keep asking until you do."

Because I can be dogged when I want. It's not easy for me to let go of something once I've set my heart on it, and now, I've set my heart on the truth.

All I have left of my mother is the memories. Her stories.

And I want them all. I want to understand how this could happen—how she could die this way.

"Your grandfather put a gun to her head and forced her to blow him. Later, he raped her."

The world tilts. The precarious ground I'd balanced on all my life tips, pitches me forward.

"It went on for years," she says.

I manage to ask, "When did it start?"

"She was ten or eleven when it started. It's why she tried to kill herself with his gun. She would've managed it if he hadn't caught her with it and taken it away."

"I didn't know she'd tried with a gun. I thought it had been pills."

The metaphorical floor may be gone beneath me, but in its place is a crystalline image.

I finally had the *why*.

Why my mother had tried to kill herself so young.

Why her mental illness had developed so early.

Why she'd failed out of middle school and had never returned. I thought it had been because her father had her selling pills at school, that she'd been caught and suspended for it. That might have been part of it, but the data also shows that sexually abused girls' grades deteriorate quickly.

It even makes sense why she developed seizures.

A 1979 article from the National Library of Medicine[1], published when my mother was sixteen, called hysterical seizures "the sequel to incestuous rape."

I can even see why two failed marriages had followed her escape.

When someone doesn't love you like they should, when your worth and esteem are so demolished that nothing but self-loathing can grow in its place, you find other people to mistreat you.

Others who will make you feel used. Unwanted. Unloved.

Because the demons you know are better than the ones you can imagine with the full force of your worst fears riding you.

"But Nana—" I begin, my hearting pounding in my ears.

"She didn't do shit. She knew what was happening and looked the other way."

No wonder my mother had felt so unheard, unseen. When I was a child and my mother was being dramatic or attention-seeking, I'd callously dismissed this as middle-child syndrome. Now, this behavior has a far more sinister origin story.

And I'm ashamed.

Not only does this information bring focus to my mother's life, but it also clarifies a few of my experiences that I hadn't really understood before now.

Once, I woke in the night to the sound of drumming. Three-or-four-year-old me got up and saw little figures marching across her pillow. Terrified, I crawled out of bed, crying, and went out into the living room, where I found my mother watching television alone.

"What's wrong?" she asked me.

I tried to articulate in that small-child way that I'd had a bad dream, that there were in fact tiny shadow people marching around in my bedding and I couldn't possibly go back to sleep.

"Go lay down with your dad," she said.

But I refused. I didn't want to go into another dark room. I wanted to stay in the light with her.

"You don't want to lay down with your dad?" she asked.

She had such a grave look on her face, one full of meaning that I didn't understand.

Then she patted the sofa beside her. "Okay. Sit with me then."

And there had been a hyper vigilance and sometimes overreactive responses to moments that could have suggested sexual abuse when I was a child. When my kindergarten teacher took me into the bathroom, pulled down my pants, and spanked me because I wouldn't stop talking in class, my mother *lost* it.

She went to the school. She threw the woman against the wall, telling her that if she ever pulled my pants down again, she was going to kill her with her bare hands.

Then there was the time I'd gotten what I'm pretty sure was a bladder infection, and my aunt Lana secreted me away to the doctor.

It wasn't until we were in the little room and she'd begun to explain her suspicions to the doctor and nurse that I realized what she thought was happening. And in its terrible way, like a self-fulfilling prophecy, all this fear that I *might* be hurt by someone actually led to real trauma.

When the doctors held me down.

When they forced my legs open and scraped around inside me for evidence that wasn't there.

I screamed. I begged. I remember being sore for days after.

I was only six or seven years old when this happened.

I have no memory of being sexually abused or touched in any way, but I sure remember that day in the doctor's office. I bear the marks of my medical terror even now.

My doctor has never been able to get a blood pressure reading under 140 when I'm in her office. For visits when I have to get a pap smear, it can easily top 160. She was so concerned, she asked me to get a cuff and test myself at home. When I reported that it had been only 108 over 69, she told me about white coat syndrome.

"Some people just get nervous in the doctor's office."

"Yes," I said. "That must be it."

And my wife didn't understand why, when I needed an MRI to diagnose my migraines, I nearly hyperventilated when they forced me to lie back on the table, to be very still, while they injected me with the solution that would light up my brain.

Why, when lying in the tube, I was paralyzed with fear, my voice trapped in my throat as terror rolled through me in palpable waves. Why I shook for fifteen minutes after.

I don't know if this is what PTSD is like.

But if it is, no wonder my mother tried to end her life. If she'd had to ride this razor edge of helplessness and terror every night she lay down in her bed, waiting for her father to come into her room.

To hurt her again. And again.

While no one helped her. No one stopped it.

Not even her own mother.

No wonder my mom lost her mind.

I PROBABLY DON'T NEED TO TELL YOU THAT I GREW UP *without* knowing my grandfather was a rapist. This was something no one—and I mean *no one*—had ever talked about.

This is the man I remembered:

Blonde-haired, brown-eyed. Gaunt, severe cheeks. He shaved daily but always had stubble. He reeked of Old

Spice. He liked to slick his hair back using these combs he kept in a strange blue solution on the bathroom sink. He smoked like it was going out of style. He liked bomber jackets and aviator sunglasses.

When he was shirtless, you could see the military tattoo on his bicep. I can't remember it clearly now, but I think there was an eagle involved.

Because he worked as a mechanic, the underside of his nails were always dark with grease.

He had a candy tin beside his white leather recliner, filled with only two things: those sugared orange slices and black licorice jellybeans.

He always lit up when he saw me. Called me "Papaw's sweet baby."

Kissed me feverishly on my cheeks.

When he had to go to the gas station, he'd let me ride shotgun in his black El Camino and always bought me a sundae from the dispenser there. Vanilla soft serve with rainbow sprinkles and sometimes a dollop of whipped cream.

Apart from the one time he lost his temper and accused me of breaking his garage window, he never hit me. Never yelled.

There was nothing to give me the impression that he was anything but a hard-working man who provided for his family, making sure everyone had what they needed.

But when I got older, I heard a few more stories.

One was about the whorehouse.

I use the word *whorehouse* not as a way to demean sex workers, but because this is literally what my grandmother called it.

When used in a sentence: "Back when your grandfather ran his whorehouse."

In one version, there were three women who lived

there, and my grandfather would send men that he met in his garage over to the house. Rough up anyone who'd gotten out of line. Take his pay cut. Sometimes he visited the women himself.

My grandmother, with a disturbing amount of affection in her voice, once told me that she'd called this "whorehouse" and one of the girls had assured her, "Oh, honey, don't you worry. He still loves you. He'll be home soon."

Then she'd become good friends with this woman.

I'd even been told that my grandfather had sent my mother over there to collect money from the women.

At the time, I'd been scandalized. Why in God's name would he do that? Didn't he think that was a dangerous place to send a little girl? With so many hungry grown men around?

Now his complete disregard for her safety makes sense.

In another variation of this story, David #3 insisted that these women weren't women at all, that most of those passing through the house had been underaged girls.

Then Shay tells me that my mother's first lesbian experience had happened there, that my mother had slept with one of the women working.

I don't know what else happened in this house, but I can imagine. And none of it is good.

Another less gut-wrenching story which illustrates my grandfather's appetites points to the possibility of a half-Korean uncle I've never met.

I was older when my mother told me that Papaw had fathered some kid when he was stationed in Korea.

The stories around this unnamed Korean woman were ambiguous. Someone said my grandfather had raped her. Someone else said she was a prostitute. That the relationship had been consensual until he was deployed to somewhere else and he'd only learned about the baby later.

Your guess is as good as mine as to which is true.

My mother had later joked, "Imagine my surprise when this Asian guy showed up at the garage and said he was my brother!"

When I pressed her for more information, she was only able to tell me a few details. "He seemed like a nice guy. Friendly. Polite. He was studying to be a doctor, I think. He just wanted to meet Daddy and see what he was about."

What he was about...*what he was about.*

I wish I could ask this man what his honest impression of my grandfather—my family—had been.

Now that I know who my grandfather *really* was, what *really* happened, I finally understand why the move back to Nashville after my father's arrest and imprisonment had been so bad for my mother.

Her drinking hadn't really been serious until we moved back. A wine cooler here. A beer there.

Then came 1988. She was almost twenty-five.

This would've been her third failed attempt to escape her father, that house, and the power he held over her, if we count both marriages and the suicide.

Three times she tried to get away, only to find herself on that doorstep, this time with a four-year-old daughter in tow.

This financial dependence on him must've reinforced all her old feelings of helplessness, of being trapped.

That no matter what she did, where she went, she couldn't get away.

I've no doubt this had been a financial decision.

With no education, she had few options.

It wasn't like she hadn't tried other things.

David #3 tells me she tried prostitution. She tried getting involved with other men who could provide a roof over her head, a place for me to sleep.

But that life hadn't been sustainable.

So she'd been forced to come home. Back to the house where she'd been a prisoner for so long.

Forced to move her daughter into the very bedroom where her own mind and body had been torn apart.

What must she have felt when she saw me, her only baby, climb onto her rapist's lap? When she heard me laughing in his arms? What had she felt when he bounced me on his knee, tickled me, or stroked my hair?

When he fed me candy from the tin by his chair, when he took me for ice cream? Took me anywhere out of her sight.

How a ticking clock must've resounded through her mind, every minute of every day.

Had it been me—drinking would've been the least of it.

It's impossible not to
open one's throat to song,
bursting, crying out,

*Look what I've discovered. Look
at what was here, all along.*

—excerpt of the poem "robins at dawn" from the
　　collection *Then Came Love*

CHAPTER TWELVE

With a more complete picture of my mother's history, I become deeply interested in trauma research. I drill my psychologist friend for what she knows about its origin and causes. I read every book I can get my hands on. *It Didn't Start With You: How Inherited Family Trauma Shapes Who We Are and How to End the Cycle* by Mark Wolynn. *The Body Keeps the Score: Brain, Mind, and Body in the Healing of Trauma* by Bessel van der Kolk. Brené Brown's *The Power of Vulnerability*, which talks about the long-lasting impacts of shame.

It's the friend with the PhD in psychology that turns me on to the Adverse Childhood Experiences study, also known as ACEs. She sends me the CDC's interactive page[1] that allows you to see how each rough childhood experience compounds your risk of long-term problems.

Types of ACEs include physical, emotional, and sexual abuse. Physical and emotional neglect. And situational household problems, such as a caregiver with mental illness, a mother treated violently, divorce, substance abuse, or having an incarcerated relative.

People who score high on the ACEs test are more likely to smoke, become alcoholics or drug addicts, miss work, or engage in low physical activity. They're also prone to obesity, diabetes, COPD, stroke, cancer, heart disease, and are even more likely to break a bone. Along with these outcomes, they are more likely to attempt suicide or suffer from depression.

The limitations of the test seem to be the lack of data on how positive experiences might increase childhood resilience, or how other traumas such as living in poverty or discrimination affect these outcomes.

I took the quiz and received an ACE score of seven.

I can only imagine that my mother's score would be at least as high. To give you context, any score of four or more is considered serious. The highest score you can get is ten.

In Wolynn's book, *It Didn't Start With You*, there is much talk about how trauma runs in families. That narratives are passed down along with your genes for at least three generations.

In one study, mice were exposed to the scent of cherry blossoms and given an electrical shock. In the next generation, when the offspring of these shocked mice were exposed to the scent of cherry blossoms, they displayed all the same physiological panic their parents had, even though they'd never been shocked themselves.

The fear had been passed along.

I don't know how far back my own family's history goes, and so I can't give a full account of our trauma record.

I know that my grandfather, born in 1927, had run away at age ten, stowing away on a train that he'd probably hoped would carry him to greater prospects.

I can't imagine *happy* children stowing away in train

cars, so we can assume what things might have been like at home.

And I was told that my grandmother's mother died when she was a baby. She'd been beaten to death by her husband, my grandmother's father.

Someone had found my grandmother at her mother's breast, her dead mother still reflexively holding her baby to her chest. It was unclear if my grandmother was nursing or just being held close by the corpse's rigid arms.

In the book *The Body Keeps the Score*, there are compelling passages about how trauma literally rewires your brain. Causes you to feel and experience things that "normal" people don't. A hyperawareness to threat and uncertainty.

I can attest to this firsthand.

I also glean another piece of critical information from this text:

Every single one of my mother's symptoms—from her low sense of self to her inexplicable bouts of rage, her mental illness, and PTSD—all of it falls right in line with the majority of women who share her background.

Even the pattern that sexually abused mothers tend to be dependent mothers who reverse the roles of mother and child, as demonstrated in all the times my mother was unable to anticipate or meet my needs and instead required that I fulfill hers.

Then there was the PTSD itself.

If you're unfamiliar with PTSD, it can cause fully immersive flashbacks. These flashbacks can come on suddenly, without warning.

When they do, your body reacts in such a complete and visceral way that brain scans will show the same psychological and physiological responses that your body experienced when the trauma first occurred.

These painful, intrusive experiences are so real, even on the biological level, that the trauma might as well be happening to you again.

We tend to think of soldiers when we hear the word *PTSD*, but van der Kolk's book argues that sexually abused children also have it, leading them to self-medicate with pills and alcohol.

All of this is compounded by the element of shame.

Shame is the erroneous belief that we are unworthy of love and belonging.

And unfortunately, sexual abuse victims have a lot of shame.

My mother probably thought things like, *He's hurting me because I deserve it.* Or *It doesn't matter that he's hurting me. There's nothing I can do about it anyway.*

Sexual abuse victims can even become confused about whether or not they consented to the acts.

Because the body betrays.

It responds to sexual contact whether that contact is abuse or not.

A raped child's body begins producing sex hormones. A rape turns on the reproductive factory, even if the factory should remain shuttered for years more.

And the abusers exploit this, twist this back on the child in a second, psychological abuse.

See, you want it. See, this is your own fault.

And what child doesn't want to make her parents happy?

To connect with the one person without whom they wouldn't receive the care they needed to survive?

All of this together—the family stories and the literature on trauma—help to illustrate the landscape of my family. Illuminate the dark soil from which I was born.

How and why my grandfather's chronic abuse had

completely and irreparably fractured my mother's mind, her spirit. Why she jumped from one abusive relationship to another. Why, no matter what I did, I couldn't liberate her from her learned helplessness.

Her shame kept her pinned firmly in place.

Learning all this is a mixed blessing. On one hand, it makes me deeply sad on my mother's behalf. How much she'd endured. How much she survived, only to have her life ended by another uncaring man.

But the truth also causes a surprising relief within me.

Something cracks open inside me.

There was a reason, I realize. For all of it.

None of the ways my mother had hurt me had been personal. She hadn't set out to ruin my childhood or break my heart.

She'd been at the center of a devastating detonation.

And I'd simply been there to absorb all the shock waves that followed that detonation.

When I tell people about my mother's past, about my past, their responses are strikingly similar:

"How are you so normal?"

"*Am* I normal?" I ask. "Because I spent four hours researching how to dissolve a body in a bathtub today. And if you could survive being nail-gunned in the head. You can, by the way. If you take the nail in *just* the right spot."

As with most questions like this, I always lead with jokes.

The serious answer is this: I may be normal *now*. But I wasn't always.

Me at twenty years old wasn't so different than my mother at twenty. In fact, I'd argue that we were on exactly the same path.

By twenty-four, I was depressed, suicidal, and bulimic. I was in hell.

So what happened? Why was I able to pull myself out a of tailspin and my mother couldn't?

This is a question that haunts me. One that I ask myself over and over again, as if I expect to wake and find that all my happiness has been a dream.

The effects of my mother's trauma followed her all of her life. They followed me too. But what about Joe?

Joe would've been five years old when his father began raping his sister. He would've been eleven when she ran away with the first husband. Those six years are formative years.

And it's a small house. The bedrooms are close together.

We can assume that he would've seen something, heard something.

He wouldn't have escaped all of that unscathed.

This says nothing of the trauma he might have experienced directly. The hardship of being raised by a man like my grandfather, of seeing his mother and sisters mistreated. And hadn't he also been sent to school with pills in his pockets? Hadn't he also taken more than a few knocks across the head?

Might he, like my mother, have developed a disorder?

Antisocial personality disorder, sometimes called sociopathy, is defined by Mayo Clinic as "a mental disorder in which a person… shows symptoms including aggression toward people, destruction of property, deceitfulness, theft and other criminal behavior."[2]

I'm not qualified to diagnose a psychological disorder, but these symptoms align with my uncle's history and behavior pretty well. The extensive criminal record and general disregard for human life.

It isn't like my uncle is incapable of kindness. Sometimes when my mother's delusions were particularly intense and she would spin lies for hours, he would sit with her. Listen to her. Show her tremendous patience in the face of her maddening psychosis.

Once, when my grandfather wrongfully blamed me for breaking a window in the garage, he slapped me hard across the face for asserting I didn't do it. It was Joe who stopped the second slap from coming down.

Joe whose face had pinched, pained and embarrassed on my behalf, putting himself between me and the hand.

Another time, when he, my mother, grandmother, and I got lost on the backroads of Missouri and the whole car devolved into a chaos of frustration as the gas tank whittled its way toward empty, he saw that I was upset by the shouting and pulled the van over to the side of the road until everyone cooled off.

He picked wildflowers with me in the ditch off the highway, putting into my hands a beautiful bouquet of purple blooms.

He could be a kind man. Or a very dangerous man.

I just don't know which one was with my mother the night she died.

I never saw my grandmother's hand come down.
It was indistinguishable
from the darkness we slept in…
I won't deny that I still don't.

—excerpt of the poem "departure" from the chapbook *Evolution*

CHAPTER THIRTEEN

In the days, weeks, months after the revelation about my mother's devastating abuse, I spend a lot of time thinking about my grandmother. I try to reconcile the woman I knew as a child, the strong woman I loved and felt safe with, against the woman who was my mother's complicit oppressor.

A co-captor.

Even my darkest memories can't bridge this gap.

Like the time she sent me and my cousin into the yard to find our own switches, so she could whip us on the living room floor while we braced ourselves on our hands and knees, for what offense I don't recall—

This is as good an argument as any to the idea that just because someone isn't cruel to *you*, doesn't mean they aren't breaking someone else apart behind closed doors.

And this is not an isolated event. According to the CDC, one out of every thirteen boys and one out of every four girls is sexually abused before they reach the age of eighteen.[1] Think on that, the next time you walk your child, grandchild, nephew, or niece into their classroom. Look out over this sea of twenty-five heads and ask yourself which four children are being raped.

Anytime I make these considerations myself, I immediately begin my search for the *why*. The *how*.

As in: *Why* didn't Nana leave her pedophile of a husband? *Why* didn't she just take the children and go? Get the hell out of there…

As in: *How* could she? *How* could she stand by and let her daughter be hurt like that?

And in this deep dive of research, it doesn't take long for me to find possibilities. Or rather a confluence of obstacles that would've kept my grandmother firmly in her place.

Just like it was important to contextualize my mother in order to understand her poor mental health, I suspected it was important to contextualize my grandmother in order to clarify her complicity.

Nana was born in 1935. That means when my mother was born in 1963, my grandmother was only twenty-eight years old and now married to her second husband. She would've been just about my age when her husband began raping her child.

So it's easy for me to say "She should've left him." "She should've packed up the kids and gotten the hell out of there."

But quickly, I must ask *how* could she have done it? By what means?

Though the sixties and seventies were full of cultural change for women in America, there were still significant setbacks.

Women were still largely expected to be wives and homemakers above all. This subservience was compounded, undoubtedly, by my grandmother's Christian faith, which emphasizes wives as subordinates to their husband's will.

Knowing what I know about her economic background and class, Nana likely didn't have friends or family that would support her and three children until she got on her feet. Most of her friends would've had families of their own with husbands who probably didn't want three more kids underfoot.

And her family was as religious as she was. They would've sent her back home to "work it out" with her husband.

So what did that leave her with? A shelter?

Homeless shelters in the seventies didn't prioritize the needs of abused women and children. For example, homeless shelters around LA in 1973, the year my mother's abuse likely began, reserved about a thousand beds for men and thirty for women. There was no mention of what a woman was to do if she had children in tow.[2]

There's always the option to go it alone, you might think. *She should just get out there, get a job, and pay her own way.*

This is what I think at first. Yet this is nearly impossible *today* for a woman making minimum wage and working full time to support herself, let alone three kids, and it was even more impossible in 1973.

First of all, there was the issue of earning a wage large enough to feed four mouths.

The Equal Pay for Equal Work Act, an attempt to close the significant pay gap between men and women, wasn't even passed until 1963[3], and even after, it went largely unenforced. This meant that the jobs that women could get were still low-paying jobs.

And even if somehow she did cobble together an income for the four of them, how was she to manage her money? Women couldn't even open their own bank accounts.

How was she supposed to secure housing?

Apartments require deposits and furnishings.

Homes require tremendous amounts of cash, or a large loan.

And she certainly couldn't get temporary help from a bank to set any of this up.

Well into the 1970s, a single, widowed, or divorced woman had to bring a man along when they filed for credit lines or loans, and married women had to bring their husbands and couldn't make any financial decisions without their co-approval.

So her first step would have been to secure a divorce, and if she was lucky, a bit of alimony or child support.

But that was a gamble.

What if my grandfather threatened her? If he could put a gun to my mother's head and force her to perform oral sex, it's not hard to imagine him putting a gun to my grandmother's head.

Did he tell her that if she left he would kill her? Kill their children?

And if she did manage to escape into the night, what if he fought her in court?

What if he tried to take the children away, calling her a liar—that she was a shrill woman who couldn't be pleased —who'd already left one husband and simply wanted to run away from another? What if he went to court arguing that he was the better financial option for the children—and he was. By then he had his mechanics business off the ground, not to mention his many side hustles.

What if the judge granted him protection rather than her and the children, something that still happens to this day? Then he would have license to rape his daughter without his meddlesome wife in the way, wouldn't he? He might have even elevated my mother from occasional assault to full-time wife replacement.

This says nothing of the conservative community to which my grandmother belonged. How would her church have treated her if they found out about her husband's habits? How would they have treated the children, my mother?

As tainted goods? Somehow poisoned? Women were still blamed for their marital failings then, and we can assume that as a second-time divorcee, it would've been no different.

But she could've simply pleaded her case that she was unsafe, that her children were unsafe, right?

Maybe not.

A 1970s ad for a Michigan bowling alley says, "Have Some Fun. Beat Your Wife Tonight[4]," offering a good sample of how cavalier the attitude toward spousal abuse was at the time. Recognizing that women needed protection from their husbands or children from their fathers didn't yet exist.

Women were expected to suffer silently in their homes well into the nineties, when marital rape finally became a *nationwide* crime.

There were some protections emerging in the seventies around the time my grandmother would've discovered the abuse, but it doesn't mean she fully understood her rights.

She was born in the thirties, in a completely different time, with her own history of learned helplessness, conditioning, and trauma behind her.

She would've come of age in the fifties and been one of those long-suffering housewives we now only see on television. She would've been told to have dinner on the table by five every evening, to wear those heels while cooking and cleaning, to always look her best. She was spoon-fed a doctrine which dictated anything happening in the home, such as a wayward husband or disobedient children, was her own fault. She wasn't to cause a fuss, and she was never to shame or humiliate him in any way, and if she was beaten for speaking up or taking a stand, well, that was her fault too.

Whatever happened in the home, stayed in the home.

"We solve our problems in the family," my uncle Joe has said more times than I can count. And where, I wonder, did he learn this philosophy?

Yet, despite all of these obstacles, my grandmother did try to leave him.

It's noted in the property records that my grandmother divorced my grandfather on October 4, 1978, only to later remarry him.

My mother would have been fifteen at the time and would've run away with David #1 shortly thereafter.

My grandmother is listed as the defendant in the divorce case, which suggests that she isn't the one who filed for divorce—my grandfather did. Furthermore, while my grandmother got the car, a 1973 Matador, he got the house and custody of the children—in this case, my mom and Uncle Joe. Renee would've been eighteen at the time.

Had my grandfather sought to get my grandmother out of the way so he could do as he pleased more easily? Or had he known the divorce was coming and filed preemptively?

It's all speculation, unfortunately.

The bottom line is we don't know what my grandmother did or didn't do. I don't know if, feeling her husband rise up in bed, knowing his intentions, she ever reached out in the dark, pulled him back, offered herself as sacrifice, forgoing her own wishes to spare the little girl in the next room.

I don't know if she saw dark looks in his eye and sent my mother outside to play.

Or, when writing her out of the will, she was thinking of her future, knowing that an inheritance of that size might disqualify her from the disability she would need all her life.

My grandmother isn't here to ask.

Regardless, I suspect the reasoning was the same.

She did *whatever she did* for love, or for financial security.

If for financial protection, this is a choice that millions of women are still forced to make today—deciding which is the lesser of two evils.

Abuse or starvation.

Your child's life or your own.

WHY HAD MY MOTHER ACCEPTED HER DIFFICULT circumstances? Why had my grandmother silenced her? Was it a matter of few options or an inability to accept the hand offered?

Possibly both.

We make these situations worse because we don't acknowledge that it's unresolved trauma that leads to self-medicating techniques like alcoholism and pill abuse. Not only do we not focus on healing unresolved trauma, on supporting people well enough to rewrite their stories, we can't even acknowledge the role of learned helplessness and the way it self-sabotages any attempt at salvation.

Learned helplessness wasn't even discovered until 1965.[5]

Researcher Martin Seligman used dogs to understand

what would happen if they experienced shocks in conjunction with the use of a bell.

Animal abuse aside, this is what he did. He placed a dog in a large locked crate and shocked it.

It couldn't escape.

Then he did this again, but with a crate that had a low fence, low enough that the dog could jump over to the other side if it wanted to and escape the shock.

But they didn't. Every time the abused dogs heard the bell that signaled a shock was coming, they lay down. Instead of jumping across the low fence and freeing themselves from this torture, they surrendered.

They accepted what was coming as if it was what had always happened and *would always* happen.

Through this experiments, the dogs learned helplessness.

They could not escape the cages even when the open door was right in front of their eyes.

They still lay down.

They had to be physically dragged to safety.

Victims all through the ages, including my grandmother and mother, have been conditioned to see themselves as helpless.

I know my mother in particular viewed herself only through the lens of victimhood, in the way she talked about herself, looked at herself in the mirror, and treated herself.

In fact, she was made a victim long before her death in 2020. She was made to believe this conditioning first in the helplessness she experienced as a sexually abused child, and again with more exploiters who reinforced this narrative within her.

That is the cycle. Her unresolved trauma caused her psychosis. Her pill and alcohol abuse were her attempts to self-medicate because she wasn't getting the help she needed to cope any other way, and when offers for escape did come, her learned helplessness kept her from being able to accept the hand offered.

My mother had nowhere else to go.

And that made her the perfect victim.

You might be thinking it's her own fault that she was killed. If she hadn't been there with my uncle, he couldn't have killed her. But again, this overlooks the tremendous detriment of unresolved trauma. Of learned helplessness. My mother was an alcoholic for so long *because* she was sexually abused. Her sexual abuse caused her depression, her thoughts of suicide, and worthlessness.

And if you're still thinking, *No, she should have more control of that. Pull herself up by the bootstraps like a good American*, remember that the next time you tell yourself no more potato chips tonight. Just say no to that third cookie or a second soda.

Self-control and self-management aren't so clear cut, and most of us know that. It's nearly impossible when what you're up against is far more terrible than a few extra pounds. When what you're stuffing down, or drinking, isn't just a few calories but an empty, insatiable darkness threatening to swallow you whole.

I don't blame my mother for her problems with alcohol and drugs anymore. And I suspect that my grandmother, though far from blameless, likely did the best she could.

I honestly don't know what either of them could've done differently in a system like this. Where addicts are arrested. Where women must choose between starvation and isolation or unthinkable abuse. Where unresolved trauma is something that's supposed to magically go away as we grow up and "pull ourselves together."

The system is the problem.

We need to change…a lot of things.

My mother, my grandmother, my family have become so much smaller in my mind. Now they are mere pieces in an enormous tapestry.

The real question: How much longer will we let this go on?

Everything hard pulled from the earth
is gathered here.

The souls rise—

smoke-white souls who
listen through the black side of twilight

for the shut
of a door, for someone come home.

—excerpt of the poem "1988" from the chapbook *Evolution*

CHAPTER FOURTEEN

My thumb hovers over the green call button on my phone. On the screen, the medical examiner's office number sits framed. My heart races, rabbiting high in my throat. I exhale slowly and make the call.

"You've reached the office of the medical examiner. Please listen as the following options have changed."

I run a hand down my face, trying to pull myself into a functional human.

I've almost managed it when a kind voice says, "Medical examiner's office, this is Sienna. How can I help you?"

"Yes, hello. I'm calling for an update on my mother's autopsy results."

"Your mother's name?"

I give her the name.

"Her date of death?"

I give her the date of death and listen to fingers racing efficiently across a keyboard, the typing sound familiar and reassuring.

You would think this would get easier with time or

practice. After all, I've been calling every week to ask for an update on my mother's case. And before you think I'm harassing these people, I am not. I was told to wait eight weeks from the date of my mother's death, which I did, and then to check in weekly for an update.

But now that we've reached the twelfth week, I know I'm going to get an answer soon. If not this week, or the next, certainly the one after.

The answer is coming, and I'm terrified I won't like it.

The line crackles and I brace myself for the response.

"Yes, ma'am, it looks like your mother's case is still pending. You can try back next week."

My heart unclenches.

"Okay, thanks. I'll do that," I say, and end the call.

I place the phone face down on the table and scratch out the words *Call the ME* in my planner. I flip the page to the following week and write the words again.

The doorbell rings and my little pug perks up, his ears erecting in the picture of vigilance. He trots after me, close on my heels, as I go to the door, seeing the mailman walking back to his truck as I pass the kitchen window.

On the porch is a box with my name on it. I use kitchen shears to cut it open, removing the excessive tape.

My heart drops.

I remove the small black container with the white sticker.

It has my mother's name on it, and the name of the funeral home.

I hadn't expected to receive her so soon. Just days ago, Katie texted me: *I got a call from the funeral home. She's ready. I'll pick her up tomorrow.*

The container, made of simple black plastic, looks like a trashcan I'd put in my car.

Inside, there's a bag of ashes, tied off, secured with a

metal tag. It has numbers written on the tag which I don't understand.

That's it.

I'm not sure what I'm supposed to feel now, with what's left of my mother, no more than five pounds, resting in my lap.

When our pug Napoleon died of cancer, I'd had to pick up his remains from the veterinarian office in a gift bag. Something about receiving him in a little tin, in a bag that looked like a present, had been so sad. I'd cried the whole way home, wiping my snotty face with my sleeve.

But here is my mother, sitting in my lap. The long and complicated history stretching out behind us has come to this.

I feel nothing.

The blue jays are bathing in the bird bath outside my window.

Two squirrels are fighting over the feeder, trying to knock one another from the pole.

And I feel...nothing. I've gone numb.

What an unceremonious end to such a life.

I put my mother back into the plastic container and put her on my version of an ofrenda. The top shelf of my office bookcase already houses the remains of our beloved pugs who passed, Napoleon and Josephine, and I think it's as good a place as any for my mother.

My mother loved animals. I don't think she minds one bit to have such company.

As I did for Josephine and Napoleon, I add a picture of her to the shelf.

Stepping back, looking at the three of them like that, I still can't cry. I thought maybe some great release would come when I finally had her with me, but there's only a cold darkness, a timeless winter night, resting somewhere in my chest.

I text Katie and thank her again for picking my mom up, for ordering the special box that she had to be shipped in, because apparently you can't ship dead people in just anything, and for all of her help.

"How does it feel to have her finally?" she asks.

"I don't know," I admit.

I do know that she would be glad to be with me, at least.

But concentrating on this doesn't make the tears come either.

Katie tells me a certain degree of numbness at receiving your mother in a Ziploc bag is to be expected.

I lift my mother's remains off the shelf, feel the weight of them.

How are you now? I wonder. *Where are you?*

I think about how many times she told me I was beautiful, the most beautiful girl in the world.

"All I ever wanted was a baby, and I wasn't even supposed to have kids," she told me. "But I had you, and you're perfect. Just *perfect*."

When I would call her and tell her I was worried about my writing career. When I'd say I wasn't sure I could do it. It was too hard.

"Are you kidding me?" she'd say. "Look at you. You're the most talented person I've ever met. Baby, you're so smart. If anyone can do this, you can. Look at everything you've already overcome. I have no doubt in my mind you're going to succeed. Honey, you've *got* this."

My mother struggled in many, *many* ways. But she left no doubt in my mind that I was loved.

It's true that she didn't love herself, and yet somehow, that hadn't impeded her from affirming my strengths, my gains. She was *always* quick to acknowledge that I'd succeeded in spite of her, not because of her.

That every win was my own.

She believed in my worth so strongly that I began to believe in myself.

Here, finally, I manage my first tear, at the thought that I will never hear her reassurances again.

Shay texts me: *Joe called me.*

To which I write: *What did he say?*

I'm surprised that my uncle Joe would call Shay. It's true that Shay was the last real friend my mom had. They would call each other and chat every few weeks. That's how he has her number, at least. And as far as I know, this is the only person my mother talked to on the phone, checked in with regularly, in the last few years of her life apart from me. But still, what would Joe possibly have to say to her?

They'd never been friends.

Hell, Shay hated him and trusted him about as far as she could throw him.

"What did he say?" I ask her, more than a little curious.

"He called to tell me your momma was dead," Shay says. "As if I didn't know!"

"Did you tell him I'd already told you?"

"No, I just let him carry on. And did he ever! He was crying and boo-hoo'n the whole time."

"About what? Momma's death?"

"He was telling me he ain't got nobody and how he's all alone now. How everyone is up and gone. I said, 'You've got two sons.'"

While this is true, I don't think he's spoken to his kids in years. They're in their twenties now. I suspect they don't want much to do with him.

"Did he tell you what happened the day she died? Did

he say anything about how it happened or what he thought killed her?" I ask, checking again to see what version of the story he's selling now.

"Said he thought it was an overdose. That he came home from work and found her on the floor."

My heart kicks.

"From what job?" She laughs. "He ain't had a job in quite a while. Can't keep one."

I think again of my mother's last letter, the one outlining her compounded stress about Joe's joblessness. How acutely aware she was that they couldn't survive on her eight-hundred-dollar income alone.

"Maybe he got a job," I offer weakly. "But if he's telling you the truth about finding her on the floor, then it means he lied to me. He told me he went into her bedroom to check on her that morning and found her."

"Not what he told me. Told me that he came home, found her collapsed on the floor, and put her in the bedroom."

I try to imagine this brotherly scene. Him picking her up off the floor, carrying her into the bedroom, laying her down on her bed. Maybe even adjusting the pillow under her head, pulling a cover over her body.

Later, when I find out from the autopsy report what her body actually looked like, this image will be shattered.

"What else did he tell the police?" she asks.

I recount for her the variations of his story, which dissolved and shifted under the detective's scrutiny.

"He's trying to tell me he was at work that day," Shay says. "But who works on the fourth of July?"

A lot of people, I think, but that isn't my problem with this story.

It's the timeline of the last twenty-four hours of my

mother's life and the fact that this "work" statement doesn't fit.

Shay is under the impression, by the way he's talking, that he was at work during the day on the fourth. But that can't be true. It would've had to be earlier—if he was at work at all.

At 10:10 in the morning on July 3rd, I received that surprise call from Joe, in which he told me to speak to my mom. When he handed the phone over after this brief announcement, I'd been confused, she'd been confused. I asked her if she was okay, trying to discern the reason for the call, but we both came up short. He seemed to have orchestrated this call for no reason other than for us to talk.

The call lasted six minutes, and it would be the last time I would hear my mother's voice.

The next morning, on July 4th, at 8:58 a.m., Joe called and left the voicemail demanding that I call him back immediately. That it was about my mother. And though I called him back at 9:41 and 10:01, he didn't answer.

I didn't hear back from him until 10:06.

We spoke on the phone until the police arrived, hearing the dogs yapping excitedly in the background.

And since we know that he was arrested on the outstanding strangulation charge at that time and spent the following weeks in jail, it's impossible for this "coming home from work" to occur any later.

So when could he have gone to work? The window is between 10:30 a.m. on Friday July 3rd and 8:50 a.m. on Saturday July 4th.

Depending on when this hypothetical shift may have ended, it means that he spent hours in the house with her —either alive or dead. That for whatever reason, he'd chosen not to call anyone.

Not an ambulance, or the police, or even me. Why had

I got a respectable nine a.m. phone call instead of a middle-of-the-night call?

Why might he have chosen not to inform me of her death until the next day?

Or was the word "job" code for some other nefarious activity?

Was he out buying or selling drugs?

Did he come home late—two or three in the morning from a drug deal—and that's when he found her collapsed?

That's still six hours of not helping her. Six hours that he spent doing...what exactly?

Or was it all a lie?

It's also possible that he was home with her the whole time.

That not only did he give her the drug that would end her life but that he waited, watching, doing all he could to make sure that his plan would work.

That it wouldn't fail.

His story keeps changing, Detective Barnes had said. *He says he thinks she got into his heroin. I think he did something to her. I just don't know that I can prove it.*

My stomach clenches.

"I don't know why he called me, crying and carrying on," Shay continues.

Maybe he's lonely, I wonder. Or maybe he's trying to find out what we think.

What we know. To gauge if he is out of the woods yet.

THAT NIGHT I FINALLY GET AHOLD OF DAVID #3, MY mom's third and final husband, and update him on what little I know. This is the first time I've managed to catch him in a few weeks.

Every time I've thought to call him, he was working.

Whenever he'd called me, I hadn't seen it until it was an obscene hour, too late to call back.

My mom met this David when I was nine months old. They'd joined my aunt Renee at the lake with some friends for a day of frivolity. He tells me that at first impression my mom had seemed shy, quiet.

That she'd drank a couple wine coolers but that was it.

She'd been an attentive and loving mother.

And though David remained friends with my aunt for many years, my mother hadn't gotten involved with him romantically until I was a teen.

As I was graduating from high school, they were boarding a plane for Vegas to get married, a marriage that would later be annulled.

Despite their short-lived union, he's always tried to do what was right by me. He's shown up for me more times than I could count. He's always helped me without expectation or complaint.

When my car broke down and I was stranded on the side of the road, he'd come and get me.

When I got pickpocketed in Barcelona, lost my cash, credit cards, passport, and was forced to bum money from my friends until he could wire me some more to Rome, there wasn't even a question as to whether or not he would do it.

When I'd needed money during college, he'd been the one I'd called.

He showed up for my graduations, my wedding, and though he stopped talking to my mother many years ago, he still calls me to check in. Asks how me and Kim are doing.

Now he listens to me recount Joe's varied stories, the implied alibis as thin as graphene.

He takes a deep drag on his cigarette and says, "I think

he killed them all. Hank. Your nana. And your momma too."

I settle down on the porch outside my house. It's chilly, but that's to be expected for a fall night in Michigan.

"That escalated quickly," I joke. But I can understand his reasoning.

My uncle had something to gain with each of their deaths. My grandfather's money and a quarter of the house. *Everything*...apparently...when my grandmother died. And my mom...well, that still remains to be seen.

Because I've put in an application—for the second time—to the Social Security Administration office for my mother's social security number. With it, I can search and see if Joe took out any insurance policies or anything like that. This is my last avenue, since her social security number wasn't on the death certificate.

Though the SSA seems to be taking its sweet time.

"You're not the first one to say so," I tell him. "Shay thinks he did Renee too. He was there at her place when she died. He'd been trying to put clothes on her body when the police showed up to the apartment. She'd overdosed naked in the bathroom, apparently."

I'm hesitant to bring up Shay. She and David hadn't gotten along. In fact, they fought in the front yard outside Shay's trailer one night. I watched as they swung around and around like kids on a playground, fighting over my mother, no doubt.

But he says, "I hadn't known about Renee."

"Yeah, apparently they'd been getting ready to go to Renee's girlfriend's mom's funeral or something. Guess her heart gave out before she got fully dressed. Anyway, Joe told me himself that he'd been trying to put clothes on her before the cops arrived so they wouldn't see her naked."

It's a strange image, my uncle trying to dress a corpse.

David exhales. "Is that so?"

"But I don't think he killed her. It doesn't fit the pattern."

I watch my breath fog in front of my face. A neighbor walks past with their dog. I flash a smile, lift my hand in a wave.

"He got stuff with every other death, money or property, but for Renee I don't think he got anything."

Or maybe he did it for the pleasure, a dark voice whispers in my mind.

Maybe the rush was enough, a way to soothe some pained and powerless part of his psyche, knowing that he could reach out and end a life whenever he wanted.

"Maybe you're right," David agrees. "But I still think he finished off Hank and Nana."

"Well, if he did kill my grandfather, we can't say the sick bastard didn't have it coming," I admit. "After what he did to my mom."

It's hard to feel sympathy for your mother's rapist.

Emphysema or poison are both terrible ways to go. Regardless of whether or not Joe is responsible, it seems like just deserts. I wonder what my mom felt about it, watching her father die.

I think it would've been hard either way.

"Not just what he did to your mom," David says. "Renee too."

My heart sputters.

"Oh god, did he rape my aunt too?" I say. A woman with a stroller looks my way. Until that moment, she'd been enjoying an evening walk through the neighborhood with her baby.

I force a smile and lower my voice.

"Didn't he have enough going on with my mom and

the freaking whorehouse? Did he really need *another* victim? Christ."

"No, not rape," David corrects me. "Renee was fat back then. And probably a good thing, 'cause nobody wanted to bother with her."

I don't open an argument on the subject of body politics with him—or point out that fat people most certainly experience rape too.

But I know whatever he's telling me is probably true.

David and Renee had been friends first, long before my mother came back from Illinois with a baby on her hip. It seems my aunt had been friends with everyone in the Nashville scene in the late seventies, early eighties. An exaggeration, I'm sure, but to hear Shay and David tell it, you'd think this was true.

She went to bars at night and the lake on her days off, when she wasn't working at a local printing company.

I'm sure she *was* popular. My aunt Renee was funny and good company. At the very least, she always had weed.

"Once we got close, she told me some things," he says.

I keep my voice low because now there's the neighbor's kid walking his large dog. I wave. He returns it. "What kind of things?"

Another long drag on his cigarette. "About how she had to watch."

My heart drops into the pit of my stomach. "What?"

"She'd wake up, see what was happening, and be powerless to stop it."

"You mean…you mean she was in the room when it happened?"

"Yep," he said. "That's what she told me."

And what reason did my aunt have to lie?

I do a quick, pathetic calculation and realize he must be right.

The house had three bedrooms. The one my grandparents shared and two to be split among the four children. It makes more sense that they'd been divided two and two by gender.

Why in the world had I assumed my mother had been alone in the bedroom?

All this time I'd been picturing *one* terrified little girl lying awake at night, waiting for the worst to happen. But in fact, there had always been two.

Perhaps I was born to survive this.
Perhaps I was born only with the ambition
to remake myself, again and again—

the way the oak remakes itself each spring.

Whether it's an acorn, dark and dormant.
Or tall and proud in its gray suit,
or cut through and hollowed.

—excerpt of the poem "lighten up" from the collection *You Can't Keep It*

CHAPTER FIFTEEN

My mother loved her sister. They didn't *always* get along. They fought as sisters are wont to do. But they didn't fight the way that my mother and Joe did.

Had you asked me a year ago, I would have guessed the relative stability of their relationship could be attributed to the fact my aunt was three years older, wiser. Or perhaps because Renee's sense of humor made it easier to not take my mother's drama to heart.

She had a way of making anything funny. No matter how dark.

But now that I know how my aunt played silent witness to my mother's chronic sexual abuse, forced to watch her little sister be raped for years on end, it explains a lot of the patience she had for my mother.

And it helps me to illuminate the signs of her own trauma more clearly.

My aunt was my mother's half-sister. She'd been born to my grandmother toward the end of her first marriage. I don't remember much about her father except that I met him once when I was about six or seven years old. He ran a church in Florida. We'd gone to St. Petersburg for a few months so that my grandmother could preach in his church.

I don't know why they divorced, or how much of a role he played in my aunt's life. But they must've been on good enough terms that he would share his pulpit with his ex-wife.

This also meant that my grandparents entered their marriage with a child each. Hank Jr. was two years older than my aunt, five years older than my mom.

I know that he'd molested my mother, but I don't know if he tried anything with my aunt or how that might have affected her.

It's possible that my mom and Renee bonded because of this environment of abuse.

One sign of this closeness between them is that my mother had wanted to name me after my aunt. But it wasn't to be.

As my mom told it, she passed out almost as soon as I was delivered—after fourteen excruciating hours of labor with no pain medicine, as she'd often liked to add.

When she'd woken up, my father had already written *Kory* on the birth certificate, the name he'd been reserving for the son he'd hoped to have.

She'd been mad as hell, but there was little she could do about it. The certificate was completed, signed, and dated. She'd at least gotten the middle name she'd wanted: Marie, which was the same as my grandmother's.

My own experiences with my aunt, with the exception of the very last time we saw each other, are positive.

In my mind, she was cool.

Not only because she wore bandanas and drove a raised Jeep, but there was just something about her. With a cigarette dangling between her lips and a sweating wine cooler in one hand, she just looked like a cool person, whatever the hell that meant to a six-year-old. She was almost always in jean cut-offs and a bikini top or tank top.

Once she took me to see *The Little Mermaid* in the theater. After it was over, as we walked through the corridor that connected the theaters to the parking lot, I was stopped in my tracks by an enormous cardboard cutout of the movie.

Ariel, Flounder, Sebastian, and the crew called out to me. All bright colors and intrigue. My jaw must've been resting on my chest.

"You like that?" My aunt was already pulling a cigarette from her pocket, slipping it between her lips.

"It's *amazing*. It's probably the coolest thing in the world. It must be a hundred feet tall!"

In truth it was about as tall as my aunt.

"Coolest thing in the world, huh?" My aunt eyed the cardboard display for a minute and then looked up the corridor.

"All right. Wait here. Don't talk to anybody, but scream bloody murder if anyone approaches you. But hey, look sad, will you?"

"What?"

"Look *sad*. Really sad."

My aunt left me in front of the cardboard display and walked back toward the ticket counter. She stopped a guy in a polo shirt who had one of those handled dustbins in one grip and a broom in the other.

When he looked my way, following my aunt's pointing finger, I did what I thought was a sad face. I can only imagine how ridiculous this looked.

Was I dramatic as a child? Yes. Was I a good actress? Absolutely not.

My aunt slapped the guy on the shoulder and headed back toward me. I thought we would just walk out then, climb into her raised Jeep and head to her place for the night. If I played my cards right, maybe I'd get a vanilla ice cream cone from McDonald's.

But instead of walking straight out the door, my aunt squatted down and picked up the display.

"Whoa. You're gonna take it?" I asked.

"He said I could. Get the door."

I must've made some high-pitched squealing sound as I ran ahead to get the door then struggled to push it open.

"Why did he say we could have it?"

"I told him you were an orphan."

"Orphaned? Like Oliver?"

Because I'd seen *Oliver & Company* the year before, about the orphaned kitty in need of a forever home.

"Yeah. And I'm the kindly aunt who's going to raise you as my own."

My aunt dated mostly women. This pattern was so predictable that when I *did* see her with a man, it was always a jarring and strange experience for me. I'm sure this image I had of her wasn't helped by the bandanas and raised Jeep, or the masculine swagger she often projected.

One of her longest partnerships was with a woman who I remember only one thing about. She drank water. *Only* water. As an adult I only drink water and tea myself, but as a child I was fully emerged in the realm of Kool-Aid, soda, and sometimes, if I was good, my grandmother's coveted sweet acidophilus milk, in its attractive yellow plastic container.

But as a child, *no one* I knew drank *water*.

It was so scandalous, we would actually whisper about this.

"Have you met Renee's new girlfriend? She only drinks *water*." As if this really was the most bewildering thing happening in my world.

Another one of her girlfriends had a daughter just a couple of years younger than me. This meant I had, at long last, a female playmate. Until then I'd had a male half-cousin from Aunt Lana's first marriage, and the two little boy cousins she'd had with Joe, freshly arrived.

I went from being an only child to the self-appointed leader of a ragtag crew. Of course, not that anyone would acknowledge me as their leader, but since I was the oldest by six months, I claimed the title nonetheless.

Together we spent warm days in my aunt's backyard, in the small above-ground pool. It couldn't have been more than three feet deep, but I would float on the surface and watch the airplanes pass by overhead, their white bellies shining in the sunlight.

This view was a guarantee since the airport was about a mile away and planes passed over her three-bedroom house night and day.

In the evenings, we would all pile into Renee's bed and watch movies.

While it's true that my aunt was patient with the kids, parrying our antics with sarcasm, she did also like to torment us.

As my cousins and I lay down in the dark watching a scary-*ish* movie, probably *Poltergeist* as it was one of my favorites, I looked toward the dark window only to discover a horrible face staring back at me.

It was pig-like with a hooked nose, snarling, with monstrous white hair shooting in all directions from the top of its head. And blood streamed down its face.

I screamed first. And a chorus of voices rose to meet mine.

Except, of course, the screams were more confused than anything at first, until I added the illuminating words "The window!", at which they grew more earnest once the others saw the face for themselves.

Then my aunt had the audacity to run back inside, mask removed, and ask us, "What's going on in here? What's wrong with y'all?" Doing her best not to smile while we tried to tell her about the monster outside.

Halloween masks and jump scares weren't her only tactics.

She would also lie face down in her pool and pretend to be dead. I'd gotten wise to this game quick, but once she did it for so long that I thought she was actually dead.

Pulling on her arms only floated her across the surface, and when I tipped her over toward the sky with much effort, her eyes were wide, lifeless, unseeing.

What followed was a bloodcurdling scream from yours truly, at which point my aunt stood up, wiped the water from her face, and said, "You could wake the dead with those pipes. Hell, you just did."

She began to laugh.

I began crying.

And I'd been at her place when my mother returned after a brief disappearance. I can't remember exactly how long she'd been "gone" or what the circumstances were, but I remembered her arrival.

I'd been sitting in one of my aunt's high-back peacock chairs, folded completely inside of it, eating a popsicle. Beside me was a tall vase with blue and gold peacock feathers protruding from it, which I liked to run my hands over when my aunt wasn't looking.

Renee told me they were too delicate to touch, and that

I'd break the feathers if I kept bending them like that. She was right. I had done this more than once, but that hadn't stopped me. Only when she'd snap her head in my direction, trying to catch me, would I turn my attention to the scroll on the wall, pretending to inspect it with the fervor of an art historian.

It was a painted Chinese scroll, with two tigers ascending a mountain.

I'd been looking at the scroll when someone knocked on the door.

Renee looked through the peep hole, grunted, and undid the chain.

My mom burst in, her stride brisk. In hindsight, it's possible she was nearing mania, or coming out of it.

"Calm down, she's right—" Renee began, but apparently my mother wasn't there to collect me.

"I need you to take pictures of me," my mother announced.

Renee twisted the lid off a wine cooler and tossed the metal cap on the countertop. "For what?"

My mom inched in close to her and raised a sleeve. A large black-and-purple bruise. It looked like a handprint to me. But to my aunt, she said, "Car accident."

A look passed between them.

Then my mother pressed a disposable camera into her sister's empty hand.

My aunt sighed and took another drink before putting the cooler on the counter. "Let's do it on the balcony. The light is better."

I rose, intending to follow them out and watch, but my mom shook her head. "Eat your popsicle, baby. We'll be right back."

Then they slid the glass door behind them, sealing me inside.

Through the venetian blinds, I watched as my mother undressed, getting all the way down to her bra and underwear.

She was *covered* in bruises.

They varied in size and severity. Some black. Some fading to yellow. From the neck down, it was like looking at a corpse.

"Christ, Leitha," my aunt murmured. "What the hell happened?"

I don't remember what my mother said in reply to this. I only remember the look of her body. The cascade of blooming colors like rotting fruit. Like something was dying inside her, rotting from the inside out.

"You look like shit," Renee added.

If someone had said this to me, I probably would've cried. But my mom actually lifted her head higher. Her smile might've been sad, unsteady at the corners, yet her gaze remained defiant.

My aunt raised the camera to her eye again, snapped another picture, before cranking the little plastic wheel with her thumb to set up the next shot.

My mother treated her body with contempt.

It was as if she wanted to hurt it as badly as she could and then look into the eyes of the bastard hurting her and say, "Is this the best you can do? It's not enough. You still can't destroy me. I'm still here."

It was probably the only way she experienced a measure of power in her abusive relationships.

Renee took another route in dealing with her trauma.

I learn about this second route when reading *The Body Keeps the Score*, by Bessel van der Kolk. In it, one patient describes how, after being raped, she'd begun binge eating. By binge eating, she'd made herself bigger.

When you're big, no one looks at you, the victim had said. *When you're big, you're safe.*

And how once these women had begun therapy and shed the weight, they felt great. Until men began to notice them again—triggering their fear and sparking off their compulsive eating habits.

In a short time, these women usually regained everything that they'd lost.

My aunt, too, had cycled with her weight over the years. I have pictures of her as a chubby kid, as a too-thin twenty-something, and as an overweight adult.

Had she eaten like this to protect herself?

With so many sexual predators around, had it made her feel safer to be big?

To hide herself within herself?

Some people suffer loudly, like my mom, the fallout and shockwaves felt for miles. They will be more than happy to pull up their sleeves and show you the scars. Show you where the world has cut them. Deep.

Then there are those who suffer like my aunt Renee.

Quietly. Voicelessly. They hide as much of themselves away from the world as they can.

They suffer with eyes wide open. Eyes they wish they could shut.

I can't bring myself to do it.
These days I'm remembering things
I understood as a child:

All that lives wants only to live free.

—excerpt of the poem "boundaries" from the collection *Birds & Other Dreamers*

CHAPTER SIXTEEN

It was December 2003 when my mother called to tell me Renee had died.

I remember the moment clearly. I'd just walked through the door after my last university class of the day and had dumped my heavy backpack on the floor. It was stuffed with my end of semester materials, because I had several major projects that needed to be done in the space of a long weekend. But first, I needed food.

Before I could decide what I would eat, my phone rang.

Through my mother's tears I heard, "She's gone. She's really gone."

"Who?"

My first thought was Nana, of course. True, she wasn't *old* old. She would've only been sixty-eight at the time. But I definitely thought she'd go before anyone else in the family. I think she'd already had the first of several heart attacks by then.

She was hardly a *spring chicken*, as they say.

My friend and roommate, Jen, must've seen something in my face, because she mouthed, *Who is it?*

I mouthed back, *My mom*, before sinking into a chair.

It would be almost three years more before Jen would meet my mother herself, see the hook-shaped scar tracing her skull with her own eyes. But already, just in the years since we'd become friends, she was beginning to think of my family as "nuts."

"Renee," my mom said. "She's gone."

My aunt? She wasn't even forty-four years old.

Shock shivered through me. "How did she die?"

"An overdose. Joe found her on the bathroom floor of her girlfriend's apartment. *Naked!* He's the one who called the police. My god, what a terrible way to go. *Naked*. On the floor."

I tried to picture Joe trying to dress her large, bloated body. It was hardly a challenge for my overactive imagination.

I listened to my mother cry, the minutes stretching on, folding in on themselves. Finally, into her sadness, I said, "I'm sorry."

And I was sorry. For my mom.

For me, I was still bitter.

My mother sniffled into the phone. "She was the only one who understood me. My poor sister."

I was thinking things like, *What did she expect to happen? I told her she needed to quit that shit.*

It had been only two years since I'd last seen Renee alive, at my grandfather's funeral. The only memory I really had of the two of us during that visit was of when I walked into the bathroom, found her loading her crack pipe, and reacted with rage. How I slapped it out of her hand into the sink. How it broke on impact, splitting into three or four glittering pieces in the basin.

How I'd screamed at her, demanding to know how could she do this with children in the house.

How could you? Do you want to die?

The way she hadn't even looked at me. Bent over the sink, her gaze down. Wounded.

Was that what she'd looked like in the last minutes of her life? Alone in a bathroom? Loading a crack pipe?

Thinking…what?

How had she gotten there? Why was her life so out of control? Wondering, maybe, why she couldn't stop?

Or something simpler?

I'm tired. What will I have for dinner? Any of the mundane things we ask ourselves during the course of a day.

But what strikes me is the resonance, the echo through time. Two years and nine months had passed, but when I'd spoken to her last, it had been in a bathroom on the day of a funeral.

Now she was dead in a bathroom, on the day of a funeral.

Maybe as she was dying on that bathroom floor, she heard my angry and accusing words. Maybe those two days, years apart, had bled and become one.

Do you want to die?

Was my grandfather's funeral really the last time I'd spoken to her?

I have a photo that looks like it was taken about the same time as the funeral. In it, my grandmother sits in a chair, holding my arm affectionately and smiling. Renee has her arm thrown around my shoulder.

It's as if we hadn't fought at all.

I don't know if this photo was taken before or after our confrontation. I can't put it in the timeline.

But I hope we'd talked after. I want her to know that I love her. That thirty-seven-year-old me understands her predicament better than seventeen-year-old me. I'm sure whatever I said that day had been hurtful. Self-righteous.

Yet now, it's no longer, *That's bad, you have to stop doing it! Now! What's wrong with you?*

Today, I understand exactly what was wrong.

Her addictions were only a coping mechanism against the pain.

She wasn't her addictions.

My real aunt was smart. Funny in a dark, sarcastic way.

She would've been a good friend, a good aunt, to have around.

I wish she could've known that.

Or at least, known that I'd forgiven her.

If only it could be so easy with Joe.

Then again, Renee never put her hands around my throat.

Joe can't say the same.

I TELL ALL OF THIS TO MY THERAPIST, THE ONE I GOT specifically to help me work through my mother's death and all the secrets that followed.

With her, I review my old fears, and my new ones.

I wrap up our latest session with, "I'm terrified of calling the medical examiner tomorrow."

"Why?" she asks. She's holding one of her three cats. I'm more than a little in love with at-home therapy sessions. They should never happen in a stuffy office again.

"It's been over thirteen weeks. They're going to have an answer. They're going to tell me...hell, I don't know. What are they going to tell me?"

"What do you *think* they're going to tell you?" she asks.

"That he killed her. They're going to say she died of a

heroin overdose, and if it's heroin, I'll know it was him. She's never used it."

"Let's assume that you call them and that's exactly what they say. What will you do then?"

What will I do then?

With the certain knowledge that he killed her?

"I don't know," I admit. "Try to convince the police to charge him. Though my confidence is really low. They've let him get away with so much. Look what they did with the strangulation charge? What's murder?"

"It's also possible that you won't have your answer tomorrow," she reminds me. "They might tell you that it was natural causes. Or undetermined. How will you feel if that's what happens?"

"Confused, probably."

"I think that no matter what answer you get, it's only important that you know what *you* believe happened."

"What I believe?"

"Yes," she says. "For your own sake, you need to reconstruct the narrative and tell yourself what *you* think the truth is. It might be the only way forward for you."

What do I think happened?

I ask myself this over and over as I find the medical examiner's number in my phone and dial it with shaking hands.

My heart pounds in my ears as I listen to the ringtone until the familiar robot voice comes onto the line.

"You've reached the office of the medical examiner. Please listen as the following options have changed."

I push the numbers. I wait.

A human says, "Medical examiner's office, this is Cherry. How can I help you?"

"Hello. I'm calling for an update on my mother's autopsy results."

"Your mother's name?" she asks.

I give my mother's name.

The line crackles.

"Yes, ma'am, thank you for waiting. It looks like the medical examiner has finished her report. Let me just get it for you, and I can read you the cause of death."

My vision darkens. I hold my breath. I listen to the swollen silence filling the line.

I was prepared to invest
months and months in this, in sitting
here with the dappled sunlight…
wanting but unmoving.

Yet I need not wait so long.

—excerpt of the poem "we see what we want to" from the collection *Then Came Love*

CHAPTER SEVENTEEN

I can't hear myself think over the pounding in my ears. My vision has gone soft around the edges, my stomach sloshing with acid.

Over my thunderous heartbeat, I ask, "I'm sorry. What did you say the cause of death was?"

"The cause of death for your mother is acute fentanyl intoxication."

"Acute fentanyl intoxication," I repeat. "Fentanyl. I don't—I don't know what that is. How did she—"

I think I've heard the word *fentanyl* before. Somewhere. But I've never heard my mother mention it. And I'm not sure what it looks like or how someone ingests it. I understand, at least from context, that it's a drug.

"It's an overdose," she says patiently.

"I—" Questions float to the surface, emerging from the twisting confusion of my mind. "Does it say if there were marks on her body? Or how much of this drug was in her or—"

She interrupts me. "Ma'am, I can't tell you any of that. I can only read you the cause of death over the phone. If you need more information than that, you can go to our website and order the full report. Just fill out the form, enter your payment information, and your request will be fulfilled in a few days."

Payment information.

"Once you get your report, read through it. If you still have questions, you can request to speak to the medical examiner who performed the autopsy. She'll be happy to go over the report with you and explain her findings."

"I definitely want to speak to the medical examiner," I say. "Can I make that request now?"

"I'll make note of it, but there is a part of the form where you must indicate your wish to speak to the medical examiner as well. So be sure to check that box when you fill out the form."

"Okay."

"Is there anything else I can do for you today, ma'am?"

Anything else?

I have a *million* other things I want her to do. Email me the report now, for starters. Then march into the medical examiner's office and tell her to speak to me.

Do anything but leave me here in this swell of confusion, trying to understand the answer I've finally been given.

"No," I tell her. "Thank you."

"Of course," she says in a somber tone. "Have a good day."

As soon as I set the phone down on the dining room table, I open my laptop. I go to the website and scroll through the pages until I find the autopsy request form.

I fill it out and check the box indicating that I'd like the examiner who completed the autopsy to call me as soon as possible and go over the report with me.

After I calm down and have a chance to consider this, I

realize it's not a bad idea that I have to wait to speak to the examiner. This will give me time to receive the report, read it carefully, and write down all my questions. I'll be better prepared for the call with the medical examiner.

Had I actually talked to her today, I'm sure I would've forgotten things, or asked the wrong questions. My mind is far from a calm, placid *sea*.

I use my debit card to pay my thirty-dollar fee and provide my email. It tells me that I will receive the full autopsy report by email in five to eight business days.

Five to eight business days.

What's five to eight business days after *fourteen weeks* of waiting, I tell myself, and submit the request.

As soon as it's off, I begin a fresh research spiral. I want to learn everything I can about fentanyl. What it is. What it looks like.

It doesn't take me long to find answers. It's a hot topic.

According to drugabuse.gov, fentanyl is a synthetic opioid similar to morphine, except it's fifty to a hundred times more potent.[1] It's a prescription drug, but it can also be made illegally. When used legally, it's taken for pain.

The reason I've probably heard of it is because the opioid epidemic consuming America has been in the news more and more often lately.

The CDC reported that thirty thousand Americans died from opioid overdoses in 2014.

In 2010, only 14.3 percent of opioid overdoses involved fentanyl. By 2017, it was 59%.

Much like heroin, fentanyl causes extreme happiness, drowsiness, nausea, confusion, sedation, or unconsciousness, as well as problems breathing.

Fentanyl is cheaper and easier to find than heroin. And many dealers use fentanyl to cut heroin and expand their profit margins.

My eyes snag on a sentence and my heart sputters.

Users or dealers may not realize that fentanyl is the drug they are using as it is often passed off as pure heroin.

Pure heroin. I wonder who I know would buy *that*.

I need to tell Shay the news. It isn't a call I want to make, but I promised to report the cause of death as soon as I found out, and that time has come. I get on Facebook, open our messenger chat, and write, *The cause of death is fentanyl intoxication. The internet says sometimes it's used as a heroin filler or mistaken for heroin, so I don't know if he shot her up with it or what.*

I will have to ask the medical examiner clarifying questions as to how the fentanyl might have been ingested. But until I have the full autopsy report, I can't be sure what those questions might be.

Three hours later, Shay replies. *He killed her then. He knew what fentanyl was and a lot of people have died from the same thing.*

She goes on to tell me about an ex-girlfriend who passed the same way because a friend tricked her and laced her weed with it.

Before I can reply to this, she's left six more messages:

Damn, damn, damn. She wouldn't have no clue what Joe was about to shoot her with. No way.

How much was in her system?

SOB. That's okay, he'll get his. Karma is a bitch.

I'm calling him now.

I've just signed in to Facebook when the last of the messages comes through:

He's saying of course she broke into the safe and must've taken them all.

Here I manage to get a word in. I think of his changing story about the safe. To Shay, I write:

Why did he tell the police he thought she got into his heroin? Why didn't he say pills if he'd thought it was pills?

Because this is a sticking point for me.

When the police asked Joe what happened, he told him that he thought she'd gotten into his heroin.

Not, *I think she took too many pain pills.*

Not, *I think she used my meth, which I'm about to be arrested with.*

He'd said heroin.

And even when he was pressed, he continued to say heroin. The drug she was least likely to take on her own.

Why?

What reason would he have to say heroin? Unless he'd been certain it was heroin...and how could he have been certain unless he knew what he'd given to her? Or at least, he *thought* he knew what he'd given her.

Shay is under the impression that he's surprised to find out it was fentanyl.

I would've been surprised too, if I'd bought enough pure heroin to kill a horse only to find out I'd been ripped off and given the cheap stuff.

I ask, *Did he say what form the fentanyl was in?*

No, he didn't say. He was in a hurry to get me off the phone, saying he wasn't there, that he'd been working. At what job? I don't know about that stuff either, she replies. *I know it's for pain. My mom had patches for her back and I know around here people are dropping like flies that are using it. But no way she broke into his safe, that's bullshit.*

Then how did she get it? I ask.

He's saying that maybe she walked down to the apartment complex at the end of the road and got herself some.

He's saying she walked down to the end of the road and bought fentanyl? With what money?

I recall Detective Barnes saying, "Joe says they had a fight about money."

Had that been true? Had my mother found where Joe had hidden her SSI and taken some for herself?

I find this very difficult to believe. My mother, who'd been setting pans on fire and forgetting what she said to me fifteen minutes into a conversation, was somehow capable of, first, finding money, then *remembering* that she'd found the money, and then she walked a quarter mile down to the apartment complex. And somehow she found someone who would be willing to sell her drugs?

It's the third condition that seems the most impossible to me. Even if we overlook the enormously questionable steps of whether or not she had the cognitive consistency to walk down the street and back alone, and not get lost, there's the fact that my mother was nearly blind.

Her vision had been terrible for years, but seeing was nearly impossible for her once she'd lost her glasses.

In May, after Nana died but before her phone was cut off, I offered to buy her new glasses, because seeing was such a problem for her. "Just go down to the Wal-Mart vision center, get your exam, and pick out your glasses and have them call me. I'll pay for everything over the phone," I told her.

Joe even promised to take her, but later left a message on my voicemail saying that he went down there but it was closed.

For whatever reason, he hadn't tried to take her again, though I'd brought it up every time I'd spoken to her.

If my mother couldn't see well enough to navigate the house she knows by heart, and couldn't think straight long enough not to set something on fire or stuff something in the freezer, how did she manage to walk down the road, accomplish a drug deal, and make it back home?

And if Joe really thought this was a possibility, then why didn't he say so before? Why go on and on and insist that she'd broken into his safe, only to later say, "Just kidding, she might've bought drugs from someone down the road?"

What?

I do a bit of research about the apartment complex down the road from my grandmother's house. Google has fifty-nine reviews for the place, with an average rating of 3.1. Several residents praise the location and the friendly staff. Others complain about maintenance issues. Only one reviewer, the daughter of a resident, paints a more sinister picture, saying that the police often knocked on doors, looking for fugitives, and suspicious-looking men loitered in the parking lot.

Is this the story I'm to believe? That my blind mother, with her newly discovered money, wandered down the street and found some "suspicious-looking" young man in the parking lot, from whom she bought the drugs that would kill her?

The only thing my mother would've willingly bought was a pill.

Let's even say she did buy a pill. And she what? Walked home with it in her hand and, despite having the memory of a goldfish, didn't forget she had it with her, or that she'd slipped it into her pocket? She didn't drop it—because if she'd dropped it, that would've been the end of it.

She would've been in the road or ditch searching until well into the night.

Hell, halfway through, she would've most certainly forgotten what it was she'd been looking for.

If she'd taken it in the parking lot, the moment she

bought it—would she have even made it home? If fentanyl is in the form of a pill or lozenge it can hit you within minutes.

So then how did she make it home in time to collapse on the floor where Joe supposedly found her?

None of this is enough to corroborate Joe's story.

Probably because the story itself isn't cohesive enough to support.

Which possibility is more likely: That Joe really didn't know what happened that day? That sure, he knew what an overdose looked like and sure, he was certain of all the drugs in the world, which one it was that killed her? That even though he had multiple drugs in his safe, it *had* to have been the heroin? And all these changing stories just reflect the wild speculation on his part, because he, like us, is absolutely flabbergasted by the whole situation.

Or is it more likely that he's lying? That when one lie stopped working, he tried another. That the changing stories are simply that, smoke and mirrors to keep us from seeing a more damning truth.

That he said heroin because he *thought* it was heroin that he'd bought. That he'd given her.

That he said overdose because he *knew* it was an overdose, because he was there, he'd seen it.

Two weeks later, Joe tries to reach Shay through Facebook, begging her to call him back, making it sound like an emergency. When she finally contacts him the next day, all he does is reiterate his story, telling Shay that he had been at work that night, that he didn't know how my mother had got ahold of the fentanyl, that whatever happened, it had been an accident.

He doesn't tell her anything she hasn't already heard.

Then why, I wonder, did he insist on calling?

Because Shay wasn't convinced. Nor am I.

She would've never taken that shit, Kory. Never, she says to me.

And I agree.

But for me, the form of the drug matters. The form of the drug is the deciding factor in determining *how guilty* Joe is for my mother's death.

Apparently, fentanyl is a highly versatile drug. It comes in pill, patch, lozenge, tablet, injectable liquid, and powder forms. It can even be put on blotter paper that dissolves under the tongue.[2]

However, I can't imagine my mother putting something under her tongue, so I discredit this possibility. There's also the possibility that she absorbed it through her skin, which can also be lethal.

But in order to achieve this, it means Joe would've had to intentionally put it on her skin or left it out somewhere so she could come into contact with it.

If it was a patch, then it likely would have been prescribed to my grandmother for pain and perhaps Joe had the patches on hand. Though I suspect that the patches are not strong enough to kill a person.

Because fentanyl can be ingested, snorted, smoked, or injected, I have to consider the vehicles Joe might have used for getting it into her body. Or, to be fair, how she might have gotten it into her body herself.

My only clue is that Joe had been so adamant that it had been heroin, and heroin doesn't come in a pill. If he was certain he'd bought pure heroin, it would've come as a fine white powder.

For this reason, I'm tempted to believe that the fentanyl was likely in a form that would've had to have been injected, smoked, or snorted like heroin.

WHO KILLED MY MOTHER?

My mother wouldn't have snorted something of her own volition, so that rules that out. I can't ask about injections until I talk to the medical examiner, who can let me know if there were any marks or puncture wounds on her body—though Detective Barnes has already assured me they didn't find any needle marks.

So how did she get a powder or liquid inside of her?

Injections aside, I can think of a few ways.

Here we go from most to least ridiculous.

First of all, soda. Stay with me.

My mother drank diet soda every day. A lot of it. I don't think she ever drank just a glass of water in her life, living instead off diet soda with ice or sometimes a coffee. Is it possible that Joe dumped some heroin in her drink when she wasn't looking? The Internet can't seem to tell me how much liquid or powdered fentanyl someone would have to put in a drink in order for it to be lethal, or even if that would work. But I can imagine him dumping in a heavy dose when she went to the bathroom or stepped outside to smoke a cigarette.

Though I can't imagine Joe having the patience to wait around to make sure she drank enough soda to kill herself, which is why this idea is the most ridiculous to me.

A slightly more plausible possibility was her cigarettes.

Because of their lack of funds, Mom and Joe smoked hand-rolled cigarettes. Because of my mom's eyes, Joe rolled those cigarettes for her. Was it possible that he laced them with the powder, filling her cigarette case for the day with enough "heroin" to sink an elephant?

This seems like a bad idea. What if she'd smoked enough cigarettes to pass out but not die?

It was far from a fail-safe plan, and surely Joe realized this. Of course, it's very possible he didn't think this through and that's why he stayed home, waiting, watching, until he was sure she was dead.

There's one other possible scenario, one in which my mother would willingly ingest powder.

My mother got bad headaches. This had been true for years.

When I was a child, she'd have me run into the gas station with a dollar bill to buy a headache powder for her. They're exactly like they sound. A small packet that you open, and on a small piece of paper is a mound of white powder. It's essentially crushed aspirin with a bit of caffeine mixed in.

But being that it's in powder form, it acts fast.

Had she had a headache? Had Joe offered her a "headache powder" to make it go away?

Maybe even handing over her diet soda so she could wash it down?

These scenarios will remain the most likely after I receive the full autopsy report five days later.

She had bleeding under her scalp.

Did Joe do that?

Did he hit her then offer her a "headache powder," or worse, a "pain pill," just to get her to shut up, to quiet down?

Did he pour apologies into her ear as he handed over what he hoped would end her suffering?

And his.

Because it is still possible that my mother would've taken a pain pill of her own volition.

I know that.

And Joe could've kept insisting that it was heroin to make himself look a little more clueless, a little more innocent.

But if Joe really had everything locked up, that still

leaves the question of how she got it. If not from him, either indirectly, left carelessly on a bathroom sink or kitchen table, or perhaps, even, left by her soda cup on the side table...or directly. Pressed into her hand after he struck her.

He was sorry. He lost his patience, is all. But really, wasn't it her own fault for riling him up the way she always does? Hadn't she learned after all these years not to do that?

See? He's a good brother. He knows what she wants and can give her what she needs.

It doesn't matter, really.

Joe was responsible for her. Legally. He agreed to that the moment he signed his name to her SSI check. And he understood her impulses well enough to lock up her pills, so he can't claim that he didn't understand the risks.

He knew the risks. The danger.

Most importantly, he was the only one bringing drugs into the house. They were his drugs. His livelihood.

In no scenario can I imagine he'd be careless with them.

You died today and when I hear this,
I step out into the dewy sunlight
to listen to the robins sing.

You died today and I move the clothes
from the washer to the dryer. I call
the dog in from the rain.

You died today and I must continue on
with this business of living.

—excerpt of the poem "mother" from the collection *Then Came Love*

CHAPTER EIGHTEEN

It's still dark outside when I untangle my legs from the thirty-pound dog sleeping on them and slip out of my warm bed. Bleary-eyed, I find the toilet. Sit. Yawning, I open my phone and compulsively check my email like every other technologically addicted person in the modern world.

One subject line stops me: *Medical Examiner Records.*

I open it, squint at the text.

Do not reply to this email message or send messages to this email address as it is only an outgoing email box. Your message will not be seen or answered.

I begin frantically rummaging through my toiletries basket, trying to find my contacts so I can actually see the smudged letters on my phone. I wash my hands, get my lenses into my eyes, and open the attachment.

I'm gripping the sink, heart pounding, when Kim comes into the bathroom, sees me, and frowns. "What's wrong?"

I look up, catch sight of my wide, panicked eyes in the

mirror. "He lied to me about how he found her. He lied to the police."

Downstairs, I set up at the kitchen table. I've got my notepad, pen, a steaming cup of tea. Chai with milk. I need something stronger than green today.

On one side of the computer screen, the autopsy report is open. On the other, a blank Word document.

I'm going to read this autopsy *at least* four or five times through, this morning alone, scraping it for every question I can possibly think of. I want to be prepared when I speak to the examiner.

I want to leave no stone unturned.

The report begins with my mother's name, Leitha. Age fifty-six. And where she was found—at my grandmother's house on July 4th, 2020. Type of death: suspected homicide.

Time of death: 2:55 p.m.

Here is my first question. How can the time of death be 2:55 p.m. when I'd already talked to the detective by then, and Joe had already found her dead that morning, at least as early as nine?

I scribble this down and move on to the narrative summary:

Reportedly the decedent was a 56-year-old white female who was discovered unresponsive in the residence by family at approximately 09:00 hours on July 4, 2020. 911 was contacted. Emergency Medical Services responded to the residence to confirm asystole.

I look this word up. Apparently, it's just a fancy word for the type of cardiac arrest that means, yes, you are really dead.

Reportedly the decedent had a history of drug use (heroin), hypertension, and mood disorder.

I write my next question: Who told the police she had a history of heroin use? Did Joe lie, or was that a mistake? I didn't know about the hypertension, but I'm not surprised. It wasn't like my mother had a great diet or anything. And the mood disorder, too, I'm well aware of.

Detective Barnes contacted the Medical Examiner's Office via pager to request a response. Due to the suspicion of a homicide, Medical Examiner jurisdiction was accepted. I, the medical investigator, responded to the residence to perform a brief body examination and document the scene with photography.

Here, I hesitate. Slowly, I scroll through the PDF to see if there are in fact photographs of my mother's corpse attached with the report. Blessedly, there are not. They are more thorough than my veterinarian, then, who accidentally sent me a picture of my dog's severed leg.

That's a story for another day.

Middle Tennessee Removal Service transported the decedent's body to the Center for Forensic Medicine for further examination. Final disposition arrangements were unknown at the time of this report.

It is signed by the medical investigator and dated at 4:59 p.m. on the day my mother died.

At the bottom of this first page are two more boxes, one with the cause of death — acute fentanyl intoxication — and another with the manner of death — accident.

I write down: *Does the medical examiner think it's really an accident? Or does this mean they don't have enough to convict him?*

Next page: it has my mother's name, sex, race, and age again, as well as the date and time of death. But it also has the date and time of when the autopsy was performed. July 6th, 2020, at 9:45 a.m.

Below this repetition of the identifying information is a section titled *Pathologic Diagnoses*. It reads:

1. Acute fentanyl intoxication:
A. Mild pulmonary congestion (right lung 310 grams, left lung 680 grams)

2. Hemorrhage in the left parietal and left temporal scalp without injury to skull or brain.
3. Layered anterior neck dissection negative for hemorrhage in strap muscles.

SUMMARY OF CASE & OPINION

This 56-year-old white female was found unresponsive, lying on her right side, in the bedroom floor of the residence she shared with her brother. Clothing was piled on her body. Her past medical history is significant for drug abuse, hypertension, hepatitis C, and mood disorder.

Autopsy reveals petechial hemorrhages on the right side of her face and in the right eye, consistent with her lividity pattern and how her body was found. A layered anterior neck dissection does not reveal hemorrhage in the strap muscles of the neck, and a fracture through the other layer of bone only is noted on the hyoid bone and does not exhibit associated hemorrhage.

JOE LIED TO ME. HE'D PAINTED A PICTURE THAT HE'D simply woken on Saturday morning, and out of concern had gone into the bedroom and had found my mother unresponsive *in her bed*. He'd made no mention of her being on the floor. Nor had he explained why he might have—bizarrely—piled clothes on top of her—and what does that even mean?

The official story, at least what's written under *Summary of Case & Opinion*, is that my mother was found lying on her right side, unresponsive.

And while I write down questions about the clothes, I also want the examiner to explain why she would have bleeding on the left side of her head if she was found on her right side.

It can only mean that her head was injured before she died, since the scalp had bled. You don't bleed after you die. There isn't a working heart to move the blood around.

It couldn't be the collapse that caused her head injury, because then she would've been found on her left side, if that was the side of her head that made contact with the floor, right?

But it wasn't. The blood pooled on the right. The possibility that she collapsed in her bedroom and simply died isn't likely.

It isn't possible that my mother fell in her bedroom, hit the left side of her head when she collapsed, and then rolled entirely onto her other side and died. Especially since most of the fluid accumulation was also on her left side.

The left lung had 680 grams of fluid and the right lung only 310. Shouldn't the right lung have more fluid if that's how it settled?

To me it seems like she was lying on her left side as she was dying. Then when she died, she was turned onto her right side, where the blood then settled and pooled.

Because if someone is unresponsive enough to fall down, they probably don't have it in them to roll over. Unconscious people don't move.

The simple conclusion to this is that Joe moved her before she died.

Is it possible she collapsed in the living room, injuring the left side of her head, and this is where Joe found her, per one version of his story? If so, the overdose was well on its way by then, fluid creeping into her lungs, beginning to drown her, by the time Joe found her. And if he'd found her and moved her, as reported in one of the versions of his story—she would've been in bad shape, with symptoms impossible to overlook.

She would've likely already been blue in the face, lips. Likely she would've been short of breath, possibly gasping.

How *curious*—that Joe supposedly saw her turn blue like this during a supposed seizure that happened months before. That he'd understood the danger then, had acted immediately and appropriately, resuscitating her, and had promised to get medical help should it ever happen again.

And yet in *this* instance, where the symptoms would've been no doubt as serious if not *more* alarming, he didn't even call an ambulance or drive her to the hospital. Instead, he carried her to her bedroom and put her…on the floor.

Then he didn't get a pillow or blanket for her, the sister he was putting on the floor instead of the bed—he piled *clothes* on top of her body.

The toxicology report doesn't show up until pages six and seven of the nine-page autopsy.

There were six substances found in the blood taken from my mother's femoral artery: 4-ANPP (positive), caffeine (positive), cotinine (positive), nicotine (positive), fentanyl (33 ng/mL), norfentanyl (2.9 ng/mL).

None of this would mean anything for me if it weren't for the helpful reference comments explaining each of the findings below the results. But even so, I have questions, and I jot them down along the margins of my notepad as I go. The descriptions explain:

4-ANPP (despropionylfentanyl) is a precursor chemical used in the production of fentanyl/fentanyl-related compounds, and is also a fentanyl metabolite and may be a metabolite of other fentanyl-related compounds.

Caffeine is a xanthine-derived central nervous system

stimulant. It also produces diuresis and cardiac and respiratory stimulation. It can be readily found in such items as coffee, tea, soft drinks, and chocolate. As a reference, a typical cup of coffee or tea contains between 40 and 100 mg of caffeine.

No doubt my mother's "item" of delivery for this caffeine was her beloved diet soda.

Cotinine is a metabolite of nicotine and may be encountered in the fluids and tissues of an individual as a result of tobacco exposure.

Again, not surprising since my mother smoked close to a pack a day.

Nicotine is a potent alkaloid found in tobacco leaves at about 2–8% by weight. It is reportedly found in various fruits, vegetables, and tubers, e.g., tomatoes and potatoes, but at a smaller weight per fraction. As a natural constituent of tobacco, nicotine is found in all commonly used smoking or chewing tobacco products, but also in smoking cessation products. Nicotine is extensively metabolized, and the primary reported metabolite is the oxidative product cotinine.

The report also notes the anthracosis in my mother's lungs, which the medical examiner will explain as normal for someone who smokes. But it can also be caused by air pollution or breathing dirty air.

Norfentanyl. This is the primary inactive metabolite of the synthetic narcotic analgesic fentanyl. The substance is known to interfere with the identity and/or quantity of the reported result: benzyl fentanyl.

Then we arrive at the fentanyl itself. *Fentanyl is a DEA schedule II synthetic morphine substitute anesthetic/analgesic. It is reported to be eighty to two hundred times as potent as morphine and has a rapid onset of action as well as addictive properties.*

It is reported that patients lost consciousness at mean plasma levels of fentanyl of 34 ng/mL when infused with 75 mcg/kg over a fifteen min period. Peak plasma levels averaged 50 ng/mL.

My mother's fentanyl level was 33 ng/mL at the time of her death. That means how much was left in her body when she died. That's not how much she ingested. That's when her body gave up. Whatever she ingested must've been much higher than that—which means her fentanyl intake most definitely rendered her unconscious, making the bleeding head from a collapse possible.

And the dose must've been truly massive. *The mean peak plasma level of fentanyl concentration in adults given an 800 mcg oral transmucosal fentanyl preparation* (which the Internet describes as a lozenge or lollipop) *over 15 minutes is reported at 2.1 ng/mL (with a range of 1.4-3.0 ng ml) at approximately 24 minutes*, the report explains.

My mother's level wasn't 1.4, 2.1, or even 3.0 ng/mL. It was 33 ng/mL. Nearly ten times the amount found from an 800 mcg lollipop or lozenge.

In 2018, the DEA stated that as little as 2–3 milligrams of fentanyl is a lethal dose for most people. And they shared a photograph of what 2 milligrams looks like. It looks like a few pop rocks beside a penny.

It's so small.

That's why "law officers and first responders are warned to wear protective clothing during known raids to prevent inhalation or skin absorption of the drug."[1]

In another photograph, I see three vials showing how much heroin it takes to kill you compared to fentanyl. It's thirty milligrams for heroin, and just the two to three for fentanyl. Side by side, it looks like a pinch of dust (heroin) compared to mere dusty residue stuck to the glass (fentanyl).

It isn't until I see this photo of the drugs side by side that I realize just how little thirty milligrams is. If it really takes so little to kill a person, then it would've been so easy for Joe to roll the lethal dose into a cigarette. And it only takes a few minutes to smoke a cigarette, so my mother likely would've gotten more than enough even if she'd only taken a few hits before suspecting that something was wrong with the taste of it.

And if Joe really did mistake the fentanyl for heroin when he bought it and gave her enough "heroin" to kill her, the aforementioned thirty milligrams, it would've been ten times more than necessary to end her life.

I'm not convinced that Joe wasn't already home, watching all of this unfold as it happened. I think he would've wanted to make sure his plan had worked and it would've hit her system quick.

But let's say for argument's sake he really did leave, maybe to give himself an alibi. When he came back and found her collapsed, my mother would've definitely been showing signs of an overdose at that point.

Is that why Joe chose to dump her on the floor, rather than put her in her bed? Because she was showing these signs of fentanyl toxicity? And if so, which ones?

Seizures? Coma-like unresponsiveness? A blue face or lips? A limp body? A shallow heartbeat? Slow breathing or gurgling sounds?

And are we to believe that when Joe "found her" he didn't recognize the danger she was in? That he didn't understand that she was dying?

Of course he did.

Joe knew what an overdose looked like. He would've recognized it immediately. That's why I don't need any more information to glean Joe's intentions that night. The picture is clear enough. Joe didn't help my mother when she was dying, because he *wanted* her to die.

. . .

I make the first two or three passes of the autopsy report with a purely analytical mind. I usually lead with thoughts instead of feelings as a first line of defense against pain.

But this never lasts because I *do* have feelings—so when I read my mother's autopsy report for the fourth or fifth time, it finally hits me.

The woman in this report isn't a mystery to be dissected. This death isn't a puzzle to solve.

This is my mom.

The corpse that the examiner is describing is my mother's.

"...that of a well-developed, well-nourished (body mass index of 23.3 kg per meter squared) white female clad in a camouflage print shirt and green shorts. The body weighs 136 lbs and is 5 ft 4 inches in length, and appears consistent with the reported age of 56 years. Rigor is present to an equal degree in all extremities. Fixed lividity is on the anterior surface of the body, except in areas exposed to pressure. Petechial hemorrhages are on the right side of the face."

The clear descriptions of her body cut open, her organs examined, my mother dismantled—none of this is the part that cuts me. What cuts me is this simple, decidedly unpoetic line:

The scalp hair is gray mixed with brown.

My mother died wearing a camouflage T-shirt and green shorts.

And her hair was gray mixed with brown. When I was a little girl, I loved to fix my mother's hair. Identical to my own: thick, unruly. I liked to gather it in my hands and brush it in long, slow strokes. Sometimes she'd let me braid her hair. Or pull it up into a ponytail.

There hadn't been any gray in her hair the last time I'd seen her alive. Our last face-to-face encounter in December 2012.

That was the year the boyfriend she'd been living with for years had suddenly died. She'd been understandably sad about it, so I'd invited her to come and visit us in Michigan—*us* because Kim and I were already living together by then.

I thought this would be fine because my mother had already been to Michigan to visit me in 2009, just three years before. Then I'd asked her to come because I was at my most depressed and was in bad shape, and like most ailing children, I wanted to see my mom.

I was suicidal and slowly weaning myself off my bulimia, but I wanted her to come because I'd thought that even a shitshow of a visit would still likely have a better outcome than if I spent the New Year alone.

But to my surprise, it was a good visit. A really good visit.

She was sober, lucid. We didn't fight. We watched TV and ate takeout. She liked how quiet my apartment was. Enjoyed walking around my campus to see where I went to school, worked.

Mostly we just talked. I was comforted just by her being there.

Sitting by the window with her glasses on, she read the journals where my poetry had been published and told me how proud she was.

"You're everything I always wanted to be. I used to want to be a writer. Did I ever tell you that?"

Her on my rinky-dink sofa, in my rinky-dink apartment that always smelled like garlic because I guess some vampire hunter lived down the hall, but it had been so nice, so, dare I say, nourishing, that I'd *erroneously* expected an equally good visit in 2012.

I knew she might be depressed, of course. Someone she loved had died.

Instead of depressed, she was in a full-blown schizoaffective episode.

For the next five nights, my mother rarely slept for more than an hour at a time, day or night. The only pills in her bag were her Celexa, but I didn't see her take it once. She came with eight pills and left with eight. She did, however, take Benadryl, which she chased with Diet Coke, saying it was the only reason she could get the little sleep that she did.

She kept smoking in the apartment even though I kept trying to get her to go outside onto the balcony because Kim is asthmatic. She refused to do this because it was December. In Michigan. And because she also refused to wear pants—or much clothing at all—I was hesitant to actually shove her out there.

She watched the movie *Bridesmaids* with Kristen Wiig and Maya Rudolph on repeat.

For the entire visit. Night and day. Five days straight.

Each time it ended, she'd simply restart the movie and begin again, laughing at all the same jokes as if she hadn't just watched it.

She broke a glass and tried to flush it down our toilet. She tore open a bag of coffee and poured it all over our new white sofa.

She had a meltdown when she found our box of recycling in the closet, telling us that we lived like filthy animals because we kept all our trash in our house. She insisted that she could, in fact, clean our house better than we did, even though she kept using the bathroom with the door open and never washed her hands.

Kim had started muttering, "Oh-my-god-she-didn't-wash. Oh god she didn't wash again. Kory, she's not washing her hands!"

My mother also tried to steal—for reasons I still don't

entirely understand—my wife's flip-flops. But only one of them, which I found in a coat pocket.

Once, I tried to go down to the store to get the coffee and cigarettes she'd asked for, while Kim was at work. I got a call from a neighbor that my mother was running around the parking lot outside our building, confused, asking for me, unable to figure out which apartment she was supposed to be in.

"Where did you go? I don't know where I am!" she yelled through the phone after my very kind neighbor let her talk to me.

"I'm at the store getting what you asked for! Why did you go outside?"

At night, when we went to bed and left her in the living room on the sofa with her blankets and pillows, she wouldn't remember where she was or what time it was. She'd turn the movie on again, turn it up ten times louder than it needed to be, and begin rushing around the apartment in a panic. She did this until I got up, went out there, turned the TV down, and reminded her where she was, what time it was, and encouraged her to take another Benadryl.

But as soon as I was out of sight, she'd forget where she was all over again.

I probably don't need to tell you that by the third night of all of this, Kim was losing her mind.

The more erratic my mother became, the more unhinged Kim became. My reaction, however, was quite different.

In the face of my mother's psychosis, I fell right into the coping mechanisms I'd used all my childhood. I became *very* calm. *Very* focused.

I spoke to her in slow, soft terms. When she broke something, tried to steal something, or started the movie for the four thousandth time, I manifested patience that I never manage to have in my day-to-day existence. Say, in five o'clock traffic.

The only time I almost lost it myself was with the smoking, because I was genuinely worried Kim was going to have an asthma attack, which is why I put my mother back on the plane when our five days were over, grieving or not.

I say all of this as a context for Joe's situation.

A stressful event—like my grandmother's death—can trigger a schizoaffective episode.

If this is what my mother had been like in the last few months of her life, maybe Joe needed no other motivation —not money from a yet-to-be-found insurance policy, or the uncontested inheritance of my grandmother's estate.

Maybe all he wanted was his own peace of mind. Freedom from the caregiving responsibilities of taking care of someone so unwell. But even if Joe thought caring for her was too maddening, driving him to the edge of his own sanity—he had no right to end her life.

And I'm probably being too generous with this scenario.

It's like he was motivated to kill her for simpler, more selfish reasons than his peace of mind.

It's weeks and weeks before the medical examiner finally calls me back. When she does, I'm lying on my sofa, flirting with a headache, my arm draped dramatically over my face to block out the light.

I recognize the Nashville area code but not the number.

I shoot upright, accepting the call. "Hello? *Hello?*"

"Can I speak to Kory please?"

"This is she."

"Hello, Kory, this is the medical examiner. Dr. Champion. I'm so sorry it took me so long to get back to you. I understand you have questions for me?"

"Yes," I say. "Yes, I do."

I move
from room to room, collecting this evidence of you.

And yet I could not point to the muscle, to a vein
or ventricle and say—*here. This is where you are.*
These are the parts of me you have touched—
because still I discover you again and again.

—excerpt of the poem "houses" from the collection *Birds & Other Dreamers*

CHAPTER NINETEEN

I leap up from the couch, moving as if I'm on fire, trying to find my laptop, my notes. I've been preparing for this call for so long that now the examiner has finally called me, I go into a blind panic.

Where is it where is it where is it—

I can't get the computer unplugged. I yank it once, twice, finally pulling the cord out of the wall...and then trip over it. I also must step over the scurrying dog, who is now freaking out because he doesn't understand why we went from mid-doze to this flurry of movement.

He barks.

"Hush, shhhh," I hiss.

"If this is a bad time—" the medical examiner begins.

"It's a good time," I'm quick to say. I don't want her to have any reason whatsoever to hang up on me. Lord knows if she'll ever call back. "It's just that I have a list of questions for you on my computer and I'm trying to get everything open. If you could just give me a sec."

"Sure."

It's a good thing that she's setting this tone of patience,

because I type my password into the computer twice and fail twice before realizing the caps lock is on.

Finally, I get my questions document open and say, "Okay, I'm ready. Can I begin?"

"Absolutely." She's got that southern drawl I've been hearing so much lately. I wonder if she's a Nashville native or from some other part of Tennessee. Of course, I don't ask as we have other, more important things to discuss.

I clear my throat. "Under narrative summary it says, 'the decedent had a history of drug use (heroin), hypertension, and mood disorder.' Who told you that she had a history of heroin use?"

"Hmm, I believe the brother told us that."

"But your report says 'needle tracks are not observed.' Was there any evidence that she was injecting anything prior to her death?"

"No," she admits. "There were no puncture wounds. I was very careful and looked very closely, between the toes and everything I could think of, but I didn't find anything that looks like a puncture wound."

"Because Joe lied," I say. "She'd never used heroin in her life. He was the heroin user."

"He did say that he thought it was *his* heroin that she'd gotten into, which we thought was strange. Both the detective and myself were concerned that he'd done something to her. His story simply wasn't adding up."

"Detective Barnes told me that he wanted to look for an air bubble or something to see if he'd injected her with an empty syringe. But when you describe the examination of the heart, you didn't make any mention of abnormalities. Does that mean you didn't find anything?"

"We did an X-ray to check for air bubbles, but we didn't see anything, no."

"According to Joe, he'd taken all her prescriptions, her

Celexa, Seroquel, everything, and then locked them up in the safe. And that she broke into his safe and got the heroin that killed her. But I simply don't believe that if she got into the safe she'd take heroin. She would've grabbed her pills, or at least something she recognized like a pain pill. Did you find any other narcotics in her system?"

"Let me check." There's a beat of silence on the phone. "I requested an expanded profile that includes Celexa, Seroquel, and essentially everything else we can think of. But there wasn't anything else in her system."

"I know that my mother liked pain pills. That's true. But I just can't believe that she would break into a safe and overlook the pills and grab heroin. That's impossible. And I feel like someone in her condition who had access to a safe full of different drugs would've had more than one drug in her when she died."

"In her condition?" the examiner asks.

"Yes, in the last four months of her life, she was having memory problems. If she really was home alone with an open safe for hours, at the very least I think she would've gone to the safe a few times, took a few different things."

"Do you know what was causing the memory issue?" she asks.

"No. It started at the end of February, after she was hospitalized. Maybe it was a reaction to her mother dying? Joe said that she went to the hospital because she took her medication wrong—the Celexa and Seroquel—and that it messed her up. He supposedly took her off everything and brought her home."

"What hospital was this?" she asks. I give her the hospital name that I think they'd most likely go to, since it was close to the house, and the approximate dates for my mother's stay.

Then I move on to my next question. "On the report,

my mother's time of death is listed as 2:55 p.m. But I'd already spoken to the detective by then."

"Oh, yes, that's just the official confirmation time," she says. "When we go to examine a body, we have to call time of death for our report."

"Do you have any idea what her actual time of death was?"

"It's very challenging to use lividity to pinpoint exact time of death." There's the sound of papers rustling. "Yes, her body was pretty warm when she was examined, but it had been ninety-four degrees in the house with no air conditioning. So it would be hard to say exactly what time she died."

My heart sinks a little at this news because it means we might not be able to determine for sure if Joe was home when she died. He could fudge the window of his alibi if he needed to, for a situation like this.

I decide to move on. "Under external examination, there's mention of a lot of bruising. A purple bruise on her left arm. A faint blue bruise on her right forearm. A red-purple bruise on her left middle finger, and a faint purple bruise on the left side of her lower back."

"Yes," she agrees. "That's quite a bit of bruising."

"Did all of this happen at the time of her death?" I ask. Because if so, then there would've been more of a physical altercation than Joe led me to believe with his "we had a fight about money" comment.

"No, it's very difficult to date bruises on the body. I can only tell you that they were in different stages of healing, so it is unlikely they all happened at the same time."

Still, as clumsy as my mother is, some of the bruises are hard to ignore. How does one bruise their own lower back?

The reminder that Joe was most certainly pushing her

around, roughing her up at the very least, pisses me off all over again.

"I'm sure it's probably the same for the scrapes on her left elbow, knee, and right ankle. They don't really tell you anything?"

"No, unfortunately," she says.

"What about the hemorrhages in the parietal scalp and left temporal scalp. What caused that?"

"She could've bumped her head really hard, or if she collapsed and hit her head on impact. It might also have happened if he moved her body."

"But the fact that the scalp bled definitely means it happened before she died?" I ask.

"Yes," she confirms.

Then I ask what I've been asking myself for months, on repeat. "If my uncle can go into her bedroom, take one look at her body and know it's an overdose, why did he see her overdosing on the floor, and instead of calling an ambulance, he moved her to the bedroom?"

"Sometimes they think that a person will simply sleep off whatever they took," she offers.

"He was with my aunt when she died of an overdose and he'd been a long-time addict himself. He would've known what he was looking at, how serious it was. But he chose to drag her to a room rather than call for help. *Why?*"

"I don't know," she says. "It's a good question."

"It's not clear if he roughed her up the night she died or not?"

"Unfortunately, no. It's not clear from the physical condition of the body alone."

"What about the hyoid bone?" I ask. Because a broken hyoid bone is a common result of a strangulation.

"I think I may have broken the hyoid during the autopsy," she says, and sounds truly apologetic about it. "I try to be very careful when I remove it for examination, but it's very fragile."

"So you don't think he strangled her?"

"No, there were no other indicators of strangulation. No bruising on the neck or hemorrhaging."

"Oh, and I wanted to ask about the clothes. It says there were clothes piled on top of her body?"

"Hold on." More shuffling of paper, and I imagine she has real-life photographs. And her response confirms this. "Yes, it looks like he covered her legs with clothes."

"Like he just piled them on top of her legs?"

"Yes."

"Isn't that a little weird?" I ask.

"Yes, we found this a bit strange."

I type her answers beneath the questions as I go, moving down the list as fast as I can. I shift in my dining room chair, trying to alleviate the ache in my hip.

"You wrote in the report, 'An old incision with hardware is identified in the left frontal and left temporal bones.' You also note hardware in the right knee."

"Yes, there were two screws in her right femur, near the knee."

"I'm pretty sure that was from a car accident," I tell her. "But the hardware in her head is from where he hit her with the glass ashtray and caved in her skull. Almost killing her."

"I see. I was curious about what had happened there."

"You also wrote, 'a whorled mass is in the myometrium of the non-gravid uterus'—are you talking about a fibroid?"

"Yes, that's correct."

"Good to know. I'll have to update my own medical

history next time I see my doctor." My humor feels weird and out of place, so I just jump into the next question.

"I want to ask you about her lungs. You wrote, 'The pulmonary parenchyma is red to purple, exuding slight to moderate amounts of blood fluid; anthracosis is noted.' And you also added under pathological diagnoses that she had 'mild pulmonary congestion.' I know she was a smoker, but I don't understand the rest of it. Are these interrelated or separate conditions?"

"Anthracosis is from breathing dirty air, or smoking. The drug intoxication would've caused the pulmonary congestion." More pages turn. "But it's weird that she has more in the left lung, because it should be more in the right lung since she was lying on the right side."

Because he moved her while she was dying, I think. *Instead of calling the ambulance like he should have.*

"I just don't understand why he didn't call an ambulance instead of moving her. He was supposed to be on high alert to her collapsing, having seizures, all of that."

"What do you mean?" she asks.

I tell her everything Joe told me. About the seizure that turned her blue, stopped her breathing. About the focus issues, that she was supposedly setting pans on fire and acting erratically.

I finish up by saying, "He was responsible for her. He went down to the SSI office and signed his name onto her checks under the pretense that he was going to take care of her. Why would you leave someone home alone who was setting pans on fire?"

"It's a very good question," she says again, this time more gravely.

"She insisted that she hadn't taken anything for a long time, not even her meds, and now she is dead from an overdose? Only one person was bringing drugs into the house, and it wasn't my mother. And you're telling me that all that was in her system was caffeine, cigarettes, and this massive dose of fentanyl, it just doesn't make sense. Is it possible that my grandmother had been prescribed fentanyl for pain and she got ahold of that?"

Because if my grandmother had been prescribed something and it had been in a pill form or a patch, my mother might have taken that, not understanding what it was. But again, she would've had to have taken a lot of it to get the 33 ng/mL reading that was found in her blood.

"It's impossible to know what form the fentanyl was in, but we do know that it was illicit," she says. "That compound, 4-ANPP, is only present in illegally made fentanyl. If it's manufactured properly, it wouldn't have that."

Then the drugs that killed my mother were definitely brought into the house by Joe. They were either given to her directly or left within reach. At the very least, this is gross negligence.

"I'm confused by why he said heroin, though," I say. "Is it possible that he thought it was heroin that he'd bought? I've read that heroin is often mistaken for fentanyl. I mean, one of its street names is 'synthetic heroin.'"

"It's possible he thought he was giving her heroin, yes. Thirty-three ng/mL is a massive dose."

My voice doesn't break until I ask her the last question on my list. The one I most fear the answer to.

"Do you...do you think my mom suffered?"

Tears spring to my eyes.

"*No*," she says, in a low, consoling tone. "Fentanyl is given for pain. She would've gotten very sleepy, passed out, and then felt nothing at all."

"What if he smothered her, just put a pillow over her face or—"

"To be honest, she wouldn't have noticed," she says kindly. "She would've been so unconscious, she wouldn't have put up much of a fight."

I wipe my eyes, close the computer.

"Well, thank you. That's all of my questions." I realize that she's been talking to me for more than an hour. I feel tremendously grateful that she's given me so much of her time.

"I'm glad we talked," she says. "There's quite a bit here that I didn't know. I'm wondering if I should change my diagnosis. I mean, the fentanyl killed her. That won't change. But I don't believe we realized how responsible he was for her. If that's the case, perhaps 'accidental' isn't accurate. Either way, I'll try to get ahold of those medical records from February. And I'll follow up with the detective and let you know what I find."

The room has fallen down around you.
The hour late.
And somewhere in this house a cold bed waits.

For now, I know only that I am lost, listening,
for the music that will lead me home.

—excerpt of the poem "woman playing the lute" from the collection *Questions for the Dead*

CHAPTER TWENTY

When I was a teenager, there were few things that I loved more than books. There was the girl I was really into, but how could *she* compare to Louie, Lestat, Armand, Pandora, and Akasha, Queen of the Damned. If you didn't spend the eighties and nineties reading Anne Rice's vampire chronicles, you have no idea what I'm talking about.

But if you did, or if you've ever been part of a fandom, you can understand the longing I felt when I touched the glossy cover of the hardback edition of *The Vampire Armand*, noted the exorbitant twenty-five-dollar price tag, and put it back onto the bookstore shelf.

It was October 1998. I was fifteen and a year away from getting my first job at Burger King and having my own money. For that reason alone, twenty-five dollars for a book—no matter how badly I'd yearned to read it—was far out of my price range.

I must've whined or lamented about this grievance in front of my mom. Or perhaps I suggested it as a Christmas present, which is often how I got my books in those days—

if our small Coffee County library didn't have a copy available.

How my wish was brought to my mother's attention, I can't say. But I remember vividly the gloriously shocking moment when she knocked on my bedroom door one evening and slipped into the room with something behind her back.

I sat up on my bed cautiously, unsure of where this was going. It was close to Halloween, after all. I was expecting a rubber spider or snake thrown in my face. Like her sister, my mom enjoyed a good, heart-stopping prank.

Imagine my surprise when what she slid into my hands was the hardback I'd been coveting for months. Crisp with its vibrant dust jacket, which I've since lost, though I still have the book itself.

"Whoa," I said, accepting it. It was heavy. "You got this for me?"

"I thought you'd like to have it," she said wryly. "Was I wrong?"

She pretended to reach for it, but I clutched it to my chest.

"Of course I want it," I said.

She laughed, her hand dropping.

In fact, I was so touched that she'd gone out of her way to find and buy the book for me.

I knew what a sacrifice this was for her. I had no illusions about our financial situation. My mother worked in a factory and Shay screen-printed T-shirts. We were hardly rolling in the dough. We shared a two-bedroom trailer. It was a nice trailer, but it was a *trailer*.

"But...it's so expensive," I said, looking up from the book.

"It's okay," my mom said, straightening. "I wanted you

to have it. But if you get hungry this week, you better just read your book!"

She laughed, but I wondered how close to the truth this was. If she was really going to skip a few meals so I could have this.

"Thank you," I said.

She leaned forward, kissing my cheeks, obviously pleased that she'd gotten the reaction she'd wanted from me.

I was already climbing into my bed, opening the book, unwilling to wait another second to begin my return to New Orleans and the sexy vampires who lived there.

My mom laughed. "I'll leave you to it then."

I looked up a few minutes later and caught her lingering in the doorway, watching me with a smile on her face.

"Enjoy it, baby," she said, before finally shutting the door.

This is the face I see, the version of my mom in my mind, as I close the autopsy report and file away the answers to my questions.

I see the mother who only wanted me to be happy.

And I'm left with only one question.

The question I'm asked most: "Kory, what do you think happened?"

THE PROBLEM IS THAT THE ONLY LIVING PERSON AT MY grandmother's house that night is a compulsive liar. It's hard to know which bits of information he told me and the police are true and which are fabricated. Did she have a seizure or didn't she? Did he go to work that night or not? Did he really lock up her pills for her safety or as a way to confuse her and muddle her mind, making it easier to manipulate and kill her? Was the safe broken by police or not at all? Had my mother really ever been to that apartment complex down the road?

But no matter how I manipulate these details, which mixture of truth and falsehoods I arrange, it still leaves me with a spectrum of Joe's guilt.

Wherever the cards fall, Joe is responsible for my mother's death.

On one end of this spectrum, my mother took a pill that she'd believed was a garden-variety pain pill and began overdosing while she was unsupervised. Then Joe came home, found her collapsed on the floor, saw her symptoms—her labored breathing, her unresponsiveness, her blue face—and chose to drag her to the bedroom and throw clothes on her legs instead of call an ambulance. Even though he knew what an overdose looked like. Knew that overdoses could be reversed if treated. Knew that if he didn't do something, he was going to have another dead sister before the night was through.

In this scenario, Joe chose not to help her, and that led to her death. In this version of reality, the most forgiving version, he's guilty of involuntary manslaughter or negligent homicide.

On the other end of the spectrum, Joe planned her death almost as soon as my grandmother died. He stopped giving her her medication, knowing it would alter the clarity of her mind and make her easier to control, confuse, and manipulate. He lied about her having a seizure, as a form of misdirection so I would suspect her health was the culprit, or to lead me to believe he was an attentive brother looking out for her, rather than planning her murder.

He called me hours before she died and orchestrated that last phone call because he'd decided that *that* night was the night he would finally enact his plan, and he wanted me to have a chance to say goodbye one last time.

The story about the safe was a lie. The possible apartment parking lot drug deal is also a lie, because he's the one who gave her the drugs. Either rolled in a cigarette, disguised as a headache powder, or maybe even a pill that he got her to take by some deceptive means. And when she began to overdose, he ransacked her room, taking anything valuable, including the jewelry I'd given her, and covered her body with clothes and closed the door, maybe to avoid looking at what he had done. Or to keep the dogs off of her.

Then he called me. He called the police.

And he told them she'd overdosed using his heroin because he thought that was what would show up in the autopsy, because that's what he'd believed he'd bought and had given her, and because he didn't think anyone could prove that she hadn't taken the heroin herself.

At *this* end of the spectrum, Joe is guilty of first-degree murder because the act of killing her was premeditated. If actually convicted, he should go to prison for life.

But where does Joe fall on this spectrum of guilt?

Kory, what do you think happened?

I…

I can't stop thinking about the phone call. That strange orchestration of Joe calling for no apparent reason, asking me to speak to my mother, as he'd never done before, and her confusion mirroring my own.

All of this just hours before she died. What timing. A hell of a coincidence.

Unless, of course, he knew exactly what he had planned.

In the end, no matter where the truth lies on this spectrum, it doesn't erase Joe's responsibility or change the facts.

My mother died with caffeine, cigarettes, and a massive dose of fentanyl in her system. She'd sworn she was clean. Joe swore she was clean. And yet, somehow, illicit fentanyl made it into the house, and into my mother's body.

The only one buying drugs and bringing them into the house?

Joe.

Whose story changed under pressure?

Who lied and said my mother had a history of heroin use and must've used heroin though there were no track marks on her body?

Joe.

Who had a history of violence against her—who strangled her, who caved in her skull—who had already expressed a complete and total disregard for her well-being and her life?

Joe.

Who moved her dying body rather than get her medical attention?

It was Joe. It was Joe.

It was Joe.

I don't know what will happen in the future. I don't know that the criminal justice system which has let my uncle slide for over a hundred other charges can be trusted to bring him to justice now. I don't know if a world which despises addicts, and women, especially *poor* women, can be counted on to protect one. Most will look at her record of mental illness and say she isn't worth it.

But she is. My mother didn't know it, but she's *always* been worth it.

The pines loomed over me as I worked, slept, prayed.
Summer came late but by way of an apology
brought lightning bugs, a spectacle, beacons

penetrating the darkness like messages
from future and past selves
determined to lead me home.

—excerpt of the poem "conversations with landscape"
from the chapbook *Evolution*

CHAPTER TWENTY-ONE

I was once on the jury of a murder trial. I, morbidly, was really into this. Unlike most people, who despise the idea of jury duty, I thought it would give me the chance to see the real-life workings of the crime world that I so often render in fiction.

The handling of evidence, the chain of command, real-life descriptions of what happened when officers, detectives, and emergency workers arrived *on the scene*.

During the course of the trial, I spent three weeks taking copious notes while sitting in the front row of the jury box. I listened to the testimony of the medical examiners, firefighters, detectives, and from this, gained a clear sense of the rules that govern a murder investigation.

It was the second time this suspect had been on trial for this particular murder, the first time resulting in a hung jury, meaning that the jury couldn't agree on innocence or guilt, leading to the case's dismissal.

This second jury, of which I'd been a part, would also be hung—though I was dismissed before final deliberation, spared the grave responsibility of having to decide someone's fate.

The reason the jury was hung twice, in my opinion, wasn't just because the details of the murder were unclear, but also because of the mishandling of evidence and the incompetence of the officers involved. One example is that the medical examiner had asked for a DNA sample from the suspect to match it to the blood found on the victim's black hoodie. And the police simply never provided it, even thought they'd already collected the suspect's DNA.

Why didn't they hand over the evidence? I guess we'll never know.

What this trial taught me was how solid a case must be in order to even make it to the courtroom, and even then, all the many ways it can be derailed before justice is served. Pitfalls abound. For example, if evidence doesn't explicitly follow the chain of command, it can't be used. It doesn't matter if it's a smoking gun with the suspect's fingerprints on it. It will be inadmissible in court. For all intents and purposes, it doesn't exist.

Because so much can go wrong even in the most clear of circumstances, and because my uncle has more than one hundred dismissed charges on his record, I'm left with an overwhelming doubt that my mother's case will ever see court or that justice will ever be served.

When I express this doubt to anyone, they always try to counter it.

They say, "You never know. The universe may surprise you."

They insist he should be held accountable for all that he's done and I shouldn't give up. A bold few even suggest that my lack of faith might be a way to protect myself from more disappointment.

They're not wrong.

Regardless of how it might shake out, whatever happens next isn't within my control.

I have only one thing left to do: grieve my mother.

No one else—not even a courtroom—can pardon my grief.

With or without justice, I have to find a way to put all of this darkness and despair behind me.

I'm reassured by countless sources that claim grieving is normal, natural, and absolutely necessary.

The University of Washington counseling service even argues that grieving is healthy. By grieving, we're allowed to free up energy that was previously bound to a person or a situation and reinvest this new energy elsewhere.

And *boy* have I expended energy on all of this: my mother, my family, this whole investigation.

Grieving isn't forgetting or wallowing in the past but realizing the importance of a loss, synthesizing that wisdom into our working intelligence, and, hopefully, obtaining newfound peace.

It's important to remember grieving is only temporary.

Even if it doesn't feel very temporary.

And if I have any doubt that I'm grieving my mother's death, I need only look at the list of grieving symptoms: difficulty concentrating, apathy, anger, guilt, sleep disturbances, loss of appetite, withdrawal, irritability, intense sadness or tears when a memory is triggered, numbness, loneliness or sense of isolation, and loss of life's meaning.

Yet being the overachiever that I am, I make a "grieving to-do list" from this research and outline the steps and activities required to work through my grief.

I do the journaling, the meditating, the talk therapy. I try to be kind to myself. I write this story, trying to share my experiences, not only of her death but also the life we shared together, as a way to contextualize my mother's story in a more cohesive way than I ever have before.

I do everything I can, and yet, when I begin to see any improvement whatsoever, I hit a wall and the pain comes back, white hot and unforgiving.

It's a voice that stops me, a relentless narrative that won't quit.

This internal critic says: *Stop crying. Get ahold of yourself. Why are you falling apart like this? You have to learn how to compartmentalize your emotions. If you can't do that, it's because you're weak. Because you're pathetic. You're too emotional, and if you don't get ahold of yourself, you're going to be just like her. Unstable. Broken. She couldn't overcome her past, her problems, and you're going to be the same way. If you're suffering, it's your own fault. It's because you can't pull yourself together. Why are you even crying about it after everything she did to you? Her death isn't the problem. It's her own fault. This sad, screwed-up world isn't the problem.*

You're the problem.

It's a voice that won't quit. Sometimes it's thunderous, other times it's more quiet. But it never leaves me. And I know this voice.

I know it very well.

MY MOTHER MET MY FATHER (DAVID #2) IN 1982. He heard about her because his mother had come home from church and said, "Davie, there's a beautiful young woman visiting our church with her mother and she has the voice of an *angel*. You *have* to come see her." And so he came to church to watch my mother sing. But by then, she was already dating my father's brother.

Yet this brother, who'd given my mother a bible with her name engraved on the cover, couldn't compare to the tattooed bad boy who rolled up in the church parking lot on his motorcycle.

Within three months of the bible gift, my parents were married. It was September 11th, 1982. He was twenty-four, she was nineteen. It was a second marriage for both of them.

By November, she was pregnant with me.

I don't remember what their relationship was like before he went to prison. I have only a handful of memories from the *before* time and, of course, what I've been told.

But in the early days of their marriage, my father worked as a building maintenance man for an apartment complex as well as an electrician. My mother stayed home with me. His childhood was also difficult. He had a physically, mentally, and verbally abusive stepmother who would beat him and his five siblings, starve them, make them do chores for hours and hours, and if they disobeyed, she would lock them in dark closets.

I vaguely recall meeting this stepmother when I was a child, and while I can't picture her face, I vividly remember her parlor, which was filled with creepy porcelain dolls. Shelves and shelves of those unblinking, glassy eyes stared back at you.

She was a Jehovah's Witness who'd forbidden the celebration of birthdays and holidays. They were very poor, so by the time my father was nine years old, in 1967, he was working as a shoeshine boy, carrying his box of supplies from bar to bar to make a bit of money for himself.

And he managed it so long as he didn't anger the drunken men who would then try to kick him or his box— or worse—sending him running out into the hot day as if his pants were on fire.

My paternal grandfather was a passive husband who didn't protect his children from this abuse. His face—

white-haired, blue-eyed, liver spots on his skin—I remember, as well as the fact he was an amazing harmonica player, which had delighted me on the few occasions I met him.

My paternal grandmother, my father's biological mother, was a violent alcoholic who once hit him in the head with a frying pan.

I'm sure it was for all of these reasons that my father's hatred for women was already well developed by the time my mother came into his life. Yet somehow she managed to harden this hatred into permanent contempt.

I don't know anything about the woman who accused my father of rape, only that it had happened in Raleigh, North Carolina, and that she might have been underage. Perhaps seventeen to my father's twenty-nine. I say *might* have been underage because it was a second-degree rape charge, which means that she was either underage or she'd been unconscious or otherwise unable to give clear consent.

Whatever the circumstances, my mother had been asked to testify during the course of the trial, and she had. *Against* him, rather than for him.

When my father spoke of his arrest and trial, which was rare, I was given the impression that he blamed my mother for his conviction and sentence. That perhaps had she not testified, or said whatever she'd said, he wouldn't have gone to prison at all.

Did my mother have a reason to speak poorly of her husband during his trial?

Maybe.

Years later, my mother would show me a picture of me, one or two years old, tearing into an Easter basket, the chocolate rabbit lying on mess of yellow cellophane as I hunted through the brightly colored grass for the smaller chocolates and treats. She pointed at that picture and said, "Right before that, your daddy slapped the *hell* outta me."

Apart from the times he supposedly hit her, he often cheated on her.

This was the sort of relationship that carried on until he was convicted of second-degree rape on August 11th, 1988. Just two days after my fifth birthday. He'd been arrested the March before.

During my mother's testimony, did she tell the jury the truth about their relationship, and my father hadn't liked it? Instead of serving as a character witness on his behalf, did she hang their laundry, so to speak, in the courtroom, thereby damning his defense that he was too good of a man to have done such a terrible thing?

Was it *only* the truth she told, or did she embellish his crimes? I admit, I wonder.

What must that have been like for her, to have her voice heard for the first time and with all the pomp and circumstance of a courtroom?

After years of being raped by her father and silenced by her mother, only to now finally have a full tribunal, a rapt court, willing to listen?

Whatever was or wasn't said in 1988, what I do know is that when my father returned from prison (he was released March 27th, 1992), his hatred for my mother was a palpable experience. The anger coming from him could be felt like heat against your skin.

He would show me the custody papers of when he "won" me from her, as if I was a prize to be taken, a means to hurt her. He was clearly proud of the fact he'd beaten her at this game of "who *deserves* to have our child more."

He was never hesitant to tell me what a bad person my mother was.

Conniving. Deceptive. A compulsive liar. A nutcase, basket case. Crazy. A whore.

Every new mistake that my mother made only solidified this opinion.

One summer, he brought me to visit her at my grandmother's. He'd been out of prison for a year or two, and I'd just spent the school year with him. I'd missed my mom during the year—this was the longest I'd ever been away from her—and was excited to see her again.

But we'd only been in the house for about thirty minutes when my father reached across the counter island in my grandmother's kitchen and squeezed my mother's arm.

I don't know why he grabbed her, but when he did, she cried out.

So he yanked up her sleeve to reveal the track marks from the cocaine she'd injected with the help of David #1 —the ex-husband who'd been leaning against his car in my grandparents' driveway when we pulled up.

I'll never forget the expression on his face when he looked up from the marks, into my mother's face.

Got you, those eyes said.

"Get in the car, Kory," my father told me as my mother began to cry. "We're going for ice cream."

He didn't let me kiss my mother goodbye. Or say anything to her before he ushered me into the car and began backing out of the long, steep driveway.

At the end of the driveway, his eyes still fixed on my grandmother's house, he said, "You know we're not coming back, right?"

"I know," I said, waving to my cousins, who stood confused in the doorway.

But my father wasn't sad for me. Nor did he acknowledge how disappointed or heartbroken I was to have my summer plans, the happy reunion I'd longed for, dashed.

Instead, he was elated.

No doubt he was bolstered by the knowledge that yet again he'd won. He'd succeeded in making my mother look and feel like shit.

Later, my mother would visit us in Illinois, where my father had rented a little house next door to one of his many cousins.

I was ten or eleven years old when she flew up to stay with us. We ran into trouble almost from the start, when my father and I arrived at the airport to pick her up and she was nowhere to be found.

After much panicked searching, speaking to the authorities and gathering what information we could, the security footage was checked, and we discovered that she'd left with another man.

I don't remember how we found her, but she did eventually end up at the little Cape Cod on the quiet neighborhood street.

That night, when I snuck out of my room to check on my mom, she wasn't on the sofa where we'd left her. And there were *noises* coming from upstairs. I might've been ten, but I wasn't an idiot.

I knew what they were doing.

The next day, after my father went to work, I crept up to his room and found my mother sleeping naked on top of his sheets. I snuck out without waking her and pretended I hadn't seen her like that when she finally came down. I thought she might be embarrassed.

Maybe she was. Almost as soon as she saw me, she began to cry.

"I came here to get back together with your dad. For you," she told me, wiping her nose and red-rimmed eyes on her sleeves. "But I can't do it. I'm sorry, Kory, I can't do it."

I watched as she began to pack up all her things. Including things that didn't belong to her. Money and clothes. Anything of value. Anything she could resell for cash.

I didn't stop her. I knew she was going to run, and that there was nothing I could do to make her stay. To make her want to be with me. So I fished a brown paper bag out from under the sink that she could put things in, and I waited on the porch with her until the cab came.

When my father arrived home from work, I told him she'd left. I don't know if he was mad that I was there by myself or if he was mad that she'd stolen his stuff.

Either way, the vehemence poured forth unchecked.

"She's sick," he said, obviously disgusted. "This is what sick, fucked-up people do. You have to stop expecting anything else from her."

It's hard to explain why I valued my father's opinions so much.

Before my father was released from prison, he'd send me drawings and letters. Micky Mouse. A unicorn. All seven of the dwarfs and Snow White painted on what I suspect might have been panty hose stretched over wire hanger frames. I assure you they were more beautiful than this sounds. I'd hang each piece of art on the wall of my bedroom at my grandmother's house, opening his packages with barely controlled excitement.

I think from these limited interactions and gifts, I developed an idea of what my life would be like when my father came home from prison. And I was excited for the day when I would have two parents again instead of one.

No one would be missing. I wouldn't have to worry if

anyone was safe. I would finally get the care and attention I craved, that I was starved for.

Which is to say expectations were probably unrealistically high when my father finally came back into my life and I went to live with him just before my tenth birthday.

It's true that he got me to school every morning. That I never went hungry and I always had my school supplies, clothes, my lunch money, a new backpack. When I wanted to spend time with my friends or buy something, I usually could. He funded my school trips, including two international trips, and bought me a car not once but twice.

When all the kids in middle school had these huge Adidas jackets, he got me one too—even though I know they weren't cheap and he was struggling to get his business off the ground back then.

One of my favorite memories is how he would pick me up from school and take me to the Dairy Queen drive-thru.

We would get vanilla milkshakes with whip cream and nuts.

He took care of me when my tonsils were taken out, soothed me when I cried over a rabbit dying. He made sure my needs were met. He was the strong, steady presence that I'd been lacking.

But this stability came with a price.

Whenever I excelled or behaved in a way that he approved of, it was because I was like him. "You get that from me" meant I'd done something right.

But when I did something wrong, if I questioned him or refused to bow and be obedient, I was just like my mother.

His criticism was near constant. If I wasn't washing the dishes the way he wanted, he would shove me away from the sink. If my sweeping skills were subpar, he'd snatch the broom away. If my grades slipped, it was because I was screwing around. If I gained weight, he was sure to comment on it.

My crooked teeth were ugly and not white enough. If I had a pimple, it was because I didn't know how to wash my face. He complained about my pigeon-toed walk and told me I asked too many questions.

One particularly memorable day, when I was twelve years old, my father picked me up from school.

Our home was no longer the two-bedroom Cape Cod bungalow that he'd started in when getting out of prison, but a large multi-level house. Four bedrooms, four baths, with a finished basement and thousands of square feet. Not to mention the full-wraparound porch.

His business was doing better, and it showed.

I don't know what I did to disappoint or anger him that day, but as we pulled into the driveway, I sure do remember what he said, the words I carried with me far into my adult life:

"I think that no matter what you do in life, no matter how well you do in school or how you succeed, you'll never be any better than your mother."

It was like a sword rammed through my heart.

Because I knew he hated her. I knew that he thought she was absolute trash, the scum of the earth. The epitome of a worthless human being. I'd listened to him degrade her for years, so I wasn't confused at all about what he meant.

This one sentence told me everything I needed to know. My father thought *I* was trash and I would *always* be trash, no matter how hard I worked to be otherwise.

This narrative of me as my mother's trash daughter

would replay between us over the years, manifesting in countless ways.

With each rebuke, I got angrier and angrier. My offenses against him became more deliberate. I talked back more, whenever he criticized me. I stole money from him a few times to hurt him because it felt like money was all he cared about.

After the third time, I stopped.

I didn't like who I was becoming. I didn't like what all this anger was turning me into. And I knew the truth of it—nothing I did would convince him to see me as my own person. Anything bad I did would only ever be because I was my mother's daughter. It was certainly never because of anything *he* had done to *me*.

In March of 2020, just before I found out my grandmother had died, I'd spoken to my father on the phone. That's all that was left of our relationship at this point—a phone call here and there. I've spent one night at his house in the last eleven years. After helping me move to Michigan for graduate school in August of 2007, he never came to see me again.

Not even for my wedding.

In this phone call, I reminded him of the ride home from school that day and how much his words had hurt me.

I don't know what I'd *expected* him to say. Maybe "Sorry. That was a shit thing to do. I was stressed over my business," or perhaps even "I didn't mean it."

Instead, he said, "That was all intentional."

When I asked for clarification, he added, "I knew how much you cared about my opinion, and I knew it would push you to work harder. To be better."

Fuck you, buddy, I thought. But seeing as I was trying to maintain a semblance of civility, I said, "Or maybe I would've succeeded on my merits alone. I could've used any of my talents or intelligence to—"

He cut me off with a resounding "No."

"No?" I was astounded that someone could be so unapologetic about what was an obvious instance of abuse.

"No," he said. "Do you *really* think that?"

Later, when my father found out my mother had died, he texted me this:

I can tell you from firsthand knowledge she's been trying to kill herself for a very long time. It's really simple. Your mom chose her path and I'm surprised she lived as long as she did. If you live life by the sword, you die by the same sword you wield. I hope to die peacefully.

If *this* is the man my mother had been married to, her tearful goodbye that day as she threw one last look at me before climbing in the cab, and then her "Kory, I'm so sorry, but I can't do it" makes a lot more sense.

It's clear that his opinion of her hasn't changed. Nor has his opinion of me, I'm sure. He will continue to believe he knows my mother, her full story.

He had no problem sending such a terrible, unsolicited text, even though he hadn't talked to my mother, probably hadn't heard so much as a whisper about her, in over twenty years.

And he'll continue to believe that my success is because of all that he's done for me. That his criticism has been anything but a debilitating handicap that I have to work to overcome every day.

Truly, that's not my problem. That's his work, if he cares to do it.

In the meantime, I have my own work.

My last real hurdle.

Whether he is in my life or not—my father's voice still fills my head, blocking me from my grief.

His words and constant disdain for my mother make me afraid to embrace her. To accept the parts of me that came from her. The negatives: The melodramatics. My deep emotions. My tender heart. All the heartbreaks I endured because of her.

By the time I was an adult, my father had me thoroughly programmed to believe that the only way to escape my family's history of poverty, violence, and mental illness was to completely and totally reject my mother—and by proxy, myself.

But this also means rejecting the good things she gave me.

Her courage. Her beauty. Her great sense of humor—particularly in the face of hardship.

Her curiosity. Her kindness. Her musical gifts. Her creativity. Her love of stories. Her open mind. Her willingness to accept anyone, no matter who they were or what they had done. She could see people beyond their experiences and feel genuine deep empathy for them. She wasn't afraid to connect to the pain of others—only her own.

She was resilient. She was loving.

She had an amazing ability to forgive.

And she gifted me all of this—and more.

Whenever I'm challenged, whenever I feel my most vulnerable and unsure of myself, it's my father's voice that fuels those fears. My father saying, *You're not good enough. You won't succeed. No matter what you do, you won't rise above this because you can't. You're too weak.*

My mother's voice is the antidote.

Her words give me the strength to go on. To get up. To try again. Her voice saying, *I love you. You're perfect. Look how far you've come. Look at everything you've accomplished so far. Look at everything I put you through, and yet you're still here. None of it broke you. Not one bit. You're the strongest person I've ever met. I believe in you. Baby, you've got this. Don't you* ever *give up.*

It's still difficult to hold these dichotomous truths.

My father could take care of me but couldn't love me. My mother loved me but couldn't take care of me.

I love my mother, but I couldn't save her.

I couldn't save her—but I did, *without question*, have her love.

In the shadow of her wildness, I was able to live free in a way I couldn't with my father, a man who consumes all the breathable air around him and leaves nothing for anyone else.

But when my mother said, "You're talented, you're beautiful, you're everything I'm not," she was wrong.

When I looked at her, I didn't see what she saw.

I saw her beautiful blonde hair and shy smile. I heard her infectious laugh and gorgeous singing voice. I saw a woman who was fun, funny, who loved scary movies and would listen to you like you were the only person in the world. I saw someone who could be broke as hell and still give someone the last dollar in her pocket.

My father was hurt, and chose to hide himself away from the world. To shut everything down and bottle everything up. To pack it all away—even if it meant banishing all the good parts too.

My mother was hurt, hurting. But she still loved.

In spite of everything, my mother chose love.

If there's anything to reject inside me, anything to rise above, it's not the parts of me that came from her. If I want to move on, if I want to heal, I have to take these fractured parts back. I must embrace all of her. And all of me.

EVOLUTION

The seamen took the boat out, roared
so far beyond the dock the water wasn't grey anymore
but the translucent blue of unsettled ice.
They dropped their nets into the water,
pulled out starfish to collect on the deck.
Once the deck was so full the planks disappeared,
the seamen gathered them in their hands, one at a time
and tore the starfish into smaller pieces.
After separating each limb, they tossed the fragments
overboard, grabbed another, and began again.
They didn't stop until the planks were clean
though wet and slick like their hands.
They did this to be rid of them, to save their oyster crop.
The men called it—*control*. At first they didn't know,
if torn from their center, leaving a remnant of core still
attached to its limb, a starfish can remake itself.
But they learned when they returned after two summers
to find thousands of stars in the water.

—first published in *North American Review*, Volume 294

CHAPTER TWENTY-TWO

MARCH 5TH, 2021, 10:45 A.M.

I compose a text message while my pug, Charley, wanders up the sidewalk ahead of me, the retractable leash stretched to its end. He pauses to piss on the side of a maple tree when I hit send.

There. It's done, I tell myself. I've finally texted Detective Barnes, who I haven't heard from since he called to give me the preliminary results of my mother's autopsy eight months ago.

I honestly don't expect to hear from him. If they were moving forward with the case, I would've heard something by now. Same for the medical examiner, who hasn't returned any of my calls either.

I'm wondering if you ever spoke to the medical examiner about my follow-up questions, or if you were able to find out whether or not Joe took an insurance policy out on my mom prior to her death. And, of course, I didn't forget the obligatory *thanks in advance for your time*.

But as Charley moves on to a rose bush across the street, Detective Barnes surprises me, even if his response is cold.

Her cause of death was overdose, accidental.

Not that I can be easily quelled. And as I cross the street to clear a path for the oncoming dogwalker—a smiley lumberjack-looking guy with his flannel, beard, and man bun, doing his best to wrangle a black Lab—my thumbs are already flying across the keypad.

Yes, I know what the official cause of death is, but I don't believe it was accidental. There are many inconsistencies, like him lying to you about her history of drug abuse. And there were no track marks or anything to suggest heroin use on her body. Not to mention he was legally responsible for her as her guardian because she was mentally unwell. If he'd found her collapsed, as he'd said in one version of his story, he didn't call 911 and instead let her die. I outlined my questions and concerns to the medical examiner, and she said she was going to follow up with you. Did she? And did you check on the insurance policy or not?

To which he replies, *After speaking with the pathologist, she could not find anything that would suggest foul play.*

No mention of the insurance policy. Maybe he has to be careful about what he does or doesn't say. I don't have those restrictions.

So he didn't move her body after finding her collapsed? There's no evidence that he moved her? Nothing in the lividity pattern or the way the fluids settled?

The typing bubble appears. *Yes, he did move her from the kitchen to the bedroom. He told me so that morning.*

A woman standing on her porch is watching me text like a mad person while my dog stomps around in her bushes.

"I'm sorry," I call out, and tug Charley along. He sits down, refusing to be hurried.

He is now king of the myrtle patch.

So he saw her overdosing on the floor. Knew she was overdosing (as he was with my aunt when she died the same way)...and yet chose not to alert the authorities to get help for her. Even though he knew she was mentally unwell, with dementia-like symptoms, and could have been in a serious physical condition?

Then, before he can reply, I add:

What qualifies as negligent homicide? Does the willful decision to let someone die and not get them medical attention when you are their state-appointed guardian not qualify?

I know I sound like a twat. I feel a little sorry for him.

After a full minute, he sends: *Let me speak with our DA's office.*

But whether or not he speaks to the DA, I can't say. I don't hear from him again.

APRIL 7TH, 2021, 4:58 P.M.

A white dove lands in my yard. I'm on the sofa in my office, writing, and I hear the familiar *coo coo coo*. I look out the window, expecting to see the gray doves that have been filling my yard in twos, fours—sometimes as many as six at a time—since my grandmother died.

But it isn't a gray dove. It's white.

I call Kim over. She says, "Looks like more of a *cream* color to me."

White or "cream-colored," there's something about the bird that sends a shiver through me. I take a video of it tutting around my yard. I send it to Katie and a few other friends. I search the Internet to find out what it might mean. Yes, I'm one of the weirdos who think animals and nature are communicating with us at all times. A white dove is supposed to represent love and peace or to serve as a messenger.

Whatever its purpose, as I watch it alight on the bird bath and peck seed off the ground, a thrill runs through me. This moment feels significant, important.

I won't know why until I go to sleep that night.

I need to preface this by explaining that, like everyone else, I picked up some weird pandemic hobbies. But while others were learning how to make bread, improve their skincare routine, or buy an outstanding number of house plants—I took up lucid dreaming.

I'd heard about lucid dreaming first in the context of Tibetan yogis. They do dream work as part of their spiritual practice, believing that it helps cultivate and expand their consciousness. If you have no idea what lucid dreaming is, I bet you've still done it. Most people experience it at least once or twice in their lives spontaneously.

Lucid dreaming is when you wake up *in* your dream and realize you're dreaming.

It happens for everyone once in a while, but some people train their minds to experience lucidity on command. They learn how to induce lucid dreams so that they can explore their subconscious and talk to different parts of their minds or, if they're a believer, God. Some even use dream work to gain resolution or closure over past trauma.

That's why I was interested in it. So I got some books, started doing the exercises, and by the time the white dove shows up, I'm far from mastery but I am lucid dreaming regularly.

In my lucid dreams I often look for my mother.

Once, a photo of her was sitting on a dresser in a dream, and I asked it, "Are you my mom?"

Nothing.

"Is she okay?"

Nada. The photo didn't move. I woke up disappointed.

Another time, I gazed into a mirror and said, "Mom, are you there? Can you hear me? Mom?"

A shadow, an outline of her, darkened and faded, darkened and faded, but she didn't fully materialize. It was like she couldn't quite reach me from wherever she was.

This went on for months.

So imagine my surprise when, on the night the white dove visits me, I have my first vivid lucid dream of my mother.

In the dream, I sit up in bed. It's my real bed, the one that's sitting in my bedroom right now. In this dream bed, my wife is sleeping beside me. Charley is even curled up at my feet.

But I know instantly that I'm dreaming because my bed is in my grandmother's house, in the bedroom where I slept when I lived there. The bedroom where my mother had been raped as a child.

The bedroom where Joe left her to die.

Because there is *no* way I'd willingly be at my grandmother's, let alone sleeping in this hellmouth of a bedroom, I instantly know I'm dreaming.

I climb from bed and wander through the dark and quiet rooms.

Nothing moves.

I reach the den at the opposite end of the house. Joe had used it as his bedroom in the past. I don't know if he still does.

I peer into this room and it's only darkness. Pitch-black darkness.

Yet I stand there on the top step, waiting for what, I'm not sure.

Then, from the darkness, a voice says, "Kory? Is that you?"

And I *know* in a flash it's my mother. I call out.

"Mom! Mom! Tell me you're okay! Please, before I wake up, just tell me you're okay!"

Because sometimes when you get excited in a lucid dream, you can wake yourself up. I'd done this countless times already.

I'm worried the same thing will happen now—that because I'm so excited to see her I'll wake up before she can answer the question I've been carrying around for the nine months since she died.

I want to know that wherever she is, she isn't suffering. She isn't restless.

She isn't full of regrets.

Above all, I *need* her to know that I love her. That I understand now. I understand everything that happened between us, and I love her more than ever.

Fortunately, I don't wake up. The dream goes on.

Now the room is bathed in light. The two white recliners I remember my grandparents sitting in are side by side, facing an old television set, the huge kind that's more dresser than TV.

My mother sits in one of the recliners.

"I'm okay," she assures me, and squeezes my hands. "I'm okay."

These aren't shallow reassurances. There is no forced cheerfulness. My mother's tone is that of someone who has been through it and yet believes that she's going to be all right.

If not now, soon.

The honesty of it unclenches something inside me.

But already, she's brushing her hands together, she's standing up.

"Enough about me. I came to talk about you."

"Me?" I don't like where this dream is going.

"You have to stop living your life as if you have something to prove, Kory. You have *nothing* to prove. Not to me or to anyone. Live your life, baby. Live it for *you*."

Then she kisses me, hugs me, tells me she loves me.

And I wake up.

I wake up crying. For a long time, I don't stop.

AT FIRST, I THOUGHT THAT THE BAWLING THAT FOLLOWED this dream for three or four days was simply a relief cry because I finally believed my mom was okay. I'd been very worried. I'd been searching for some kind of connection and reassurance for months, and finally I had it.

Wherever she was, she was all right. Or she would be.

But the more I think about it, the more I wonder if I was also relieved because my mother came back not to tell me *she* was okay—but to tell me *I'm* okay.

After everything, *I* am okay.

After years and years of not believing it possible—I'm *really, truly okay*.

What I'm left with is all the steps I must take to convince myself it's true.

My mother wants me to make that journey. She wanted to give me permission to stop worrying. To stop fretting over my every move and hustling with my every breath.

She wanted to pardon me from the responsibility of hunting Joe to the ends of the earth, for demanding justice with every minute and dime I have. Of spending the rest of my life trying to do right by her, so that she would know *someone* on this god-forsaken rock loved her. *Someone* was willing to fight for her even if no one else would.

She wants me to let go. She wants me to be free, happy.

And she'll get her wish—mostly.

I'm never going to stop talking about what Joe did. I won't stop speaking out against what happened and how we should do more to help people like her.

I still feel the need to prove that she mattered—her and everyone like her.

But I also won't carry our story like a stone in my guts. My mother's story and death won't be a burden.

I can do that because of *how* my mother died. If my mother had died quietly in her sleep in fifteen or twenty years, I would never have been so compelled to hunt for the truth.

Maybe there would be no one left to tell it to me—neither David #3 nor Shay are young—but also because I wouldn't have been so desperate for answers and understanding if I hadn't been drowning in confusion.

For this reason alone, her death—as heartbreaking as it is—is a sort of gift.

It was a chance to heal all the pain I'd carried in my heart from growing up with a mother like mine. In a family like mine.

It's like I had been walking for miles and miles (my entire adult life) with glass in my feet. The skin had healed over, but the steps were still sharp.

Learning about my mom's past, understanding the detonation event that tore my family apart, removed all of that glass. More importantly, it removed the beliefs I've always carried around it:

I wasn't enough.

As a child, I wasn't enough to make her live straight and be well. As an adult, I wasn't enough to save her.

Now I know none of that is true.

It was never true.

JUNE 8TH, 2021, 09:31 A.M.

I've received several phone calls from my uncle Joe's attorney, spread out over the course of a week. I don't answer my phone when people call me, so all he could do was leave messages. As I step out onto my front porch and sit on the concrete stoop, I call him back. I'm not particularly interested in hearing what he has to say—I only want the calls to stop.

"Yes, thank you for getting back to me," he says in an upbeat tone.

"What can I do for you?"

"I'm calling because I am the representative for your grandmother's estate, and we have a buyer for the house. Joe is very motivated to sell it—"

I bet he is.

"—but the title company won't release the title unless you sign a quitclaim deed."

I frown. "How can I quitclaim to a piece of property that I haven't inherited?"

Because I saw my grandmother's will. She clearly left everything to Joe.

"You have two years from the date of your grandmother's death to contest the will. The company that holds the title on the house wants assurances that you won't do that before they allow your uncle to sell the house. Would you be willing to sign the quitclaim?"

I've already decided not to contest the will. I have neither the money, time, nor mental energy for such an endeavor. And while I can't force the justice system to do right by my mother, I'll also be damned if I'm going to help my uncle cash in on the inheritance he probably killed her for.

"No," I say.

A beat of silence.

"May I ask why?" the lawyer says.

"Because I believe he's responsible for my mother's death, and I won't be helping him in any way." *Please don't ask me to* is what I don't say, because that voice is quieter, and sadder than the one I'm presently using.

"Oh," the lawyer says. "I'm so sorry, I had no idea that was the situation."

Here, at least he is sympathetic and seems to respect my decision. He doesn't press me to sign anything, nor does he call me again, trying to get me to comply with some demand.

"May I mail you some things then?" he asks.

"That's fine." What else could I say?

I hang up, but I'm still left with this sick feeling. Now more than ever, I don't believe it's a coincidence that Joe waited until my mother was dead to begin dissolving my grandmother's estate.

For four months after my grandmother died, mom and Joe struggled for money. They couldn't pay the mortgage or their bills. They *needed* that money, and yet Joe held off until she was dead before starting the probate process.

I don't know what he stood to gain—or what he *thought* he stood to gain. Maybe he was worried she would contest it? Maybe he thought the state would seize half for her and put it in trust before institutionalizing her?

Or maybe he knew he wanted to sell and leave that house and he didn't want to take her with him.

Whatever his reasoning, it feels like he planned this.

If he did, it's worked out pretty well for him. Apart from those measly three weeks in jail between the arrest and court date, he's seen no consequences.

Joe is getting away with it.

AUGUST 5TH, 2021, 12:29 P.M.

I'm editing, trying to decide whether or not the sentence I've written can be read and actually understood by another human being, when my phone rings. It's a Nashville number. I can't tell at first glance if it might be Joe or his attorney, but those are the only two people who would call me from Nashville anymore.

I let it go to voicemail.

I continue on with editing as if nothing has happened, but in fact, my heart is pounding. My mind is trying to talk me down, back into sanity: *easy now. Whatever he wants it can wait. No need to stop what you're doing just to return a call. It's probably just more bullshit. A few more minutes won't change that.*

I calmly finish the chapter, close my computer, and then listen to the voicemail.

"Hello, Kory. This is Joe's attorney. We've spoke a couple of months before about the estate of your grandmother. I have some news to pass along to you and it's very urgent. So if you could give me a call back, I'd really appreciate it. You can reach me any time at 615…"

I press the little phone icon and listen to the slow trill in my ear.

A man answers.

"Hi, this is Kory," I say by way of hello.

"Yes, thank you for getting back to me," he says. Then his throat clicks. "I called to let you know—well, I'm sorry to say—your uncle is dead."

Silence through the line.

A stone is dropped into a dark lake.

"I'm sorry?" I say.

"Your uncle was found dead at your grandmother's house either yesterday or the day before. I thought you should know."

Yesterday? Yesterday would've been Joe's 53rd birthday, if he'd been alive to see it.

I'm trying to pull air into my lungs while my mind, blown apart, races in ten directions at once.

"Can I—can I ask what happened?"

Because I haven't forgotten my mother's hushed account of the battered face and bruises. Was he murdered? Was it a drug deal gone wrong?

"It looks like an overdose," the lawyer said. "He'd been in jail for the last six months for a drug charge. On Monday he got out on bail and went back to the house. Someone who'd been checking on the place found him, collapsed on the floor."

Collapsed on the floor.

Just way my mother had been found.

And six months in jail before that? I had no idea.

I thank the attorney for letting me know and assure him that I'll reach out to Joe's son so they can continue on with the estate.

Good, I think. *Let it all go to his kids.*

Joe's boys had lived longer and suffered more in that house than I did. It should go to them.

I get on my computer and search for Joe's latest drug charge. It takes me a while to find it because it wasn't in Davidson County. It was in Marshall.

What were you doing down there? I wonder.

Whatever it was, Joe was picked up by the Tennessee State Patrol on January 15, 2021. All this time I thought he was in that house, enjoying the prospects of a fat payday and promising new life.

But no. He'd been locked up.

His mugshot makes my heart hurt. His dark eyes are small and set in a scrunched face.

He doesn't look like a villain. Certainly not the man I've imagined coming to my house a hundred times, hiding behind my shower curtain or under my bed until I'm asleep, only to emerge from the darkness and wrap his hands around my throat.

No, certainly not the nightmare I've been imagining.

He looks like someone I'd see on the corner downtown. Someone who'd ask me for some spare change. Rough. With a deep gash in his forehead and lips that turn downward in a permanent frown. Marshall County is the opposite direction of my house.

As I look at those sunken eyes, I consider all I wished for in the last thirteen months since my mother died.

How many times I thought *he's getting away with it, he's getting away with it…how…why…*

And the anger that followed, threatening to swallow me whole and burn me alive from the inside out.

In those moments, I had wanted Joe to spend the rest of his life in jail.

I'd hoped Joe would never see a penny from that estate.

More than once, when I'd been convinced he'd left my mother on the floor to choke, gasp and wheeze out her last, I'd wished the same death on him.

That he die alone, miserable, without a soul in the world to pull him back from the brink.

I'd wished for all of that.

Then he goes to jail for the last six and a half months of his life and dies before the house is even out of probate. He was found on the floor just as my mother was. Maybe we'll even find fentanyl in his blood.

Be careful what you wish for.

I take a long weekend off to think about all of this. Not

just to figure out how I feel about Joe's death, but also to consider larger more complex questions.

Was this justice? A coincidence? Did—dare I say it—God get involved? Or a god, an angel, a flying spaghetti monster? If so, what are the implications?

Had Joe meant to die? Had his loneliness or guilt grown to such an unbearable size after thirteen months on his own that he no longer wanted to be in the world? Or was it an accident?

Had his tolerance dropped while he was in jail and as soon as he was out, he simply took more than his body could handle?

How strange it is to find myself asking the same questions about the circumstances of Joe's death, that I'd asked when my mother died.

And my feelings—*my god*, the feelings.

What is this? I ask over and over again. *What is this that I'm feeling?*

There's the relief, sure. The sadness and pity. Also an entertaining panic. *What will I do now instead of worrying about him?*

But aside from all of that, there's something else. Something ineffable.

As the tears stream down my face I try to pin it in place. Bring it to light. Name it.

It feels like both a death and a birth unfolding at once. One part collapsing. Another expanding.

It feels like I'm slowly opening my hand to let go of something I want to hold on to.

It feels like courage. The heart dilating, as I take a step off the sunlit path.

It feels like I'm looking my worst enemy in the eyes and I'm seeing—only myself.

Stripped of all the blessings that make my life beautiful.

Meanwhile I'm here. Safe. Loved.

And so grateful.

Forgiveness, I realize. *This is what forgiveness feels like.*

Like a heart that's been broken open—and yet is still so happy to be alive.

I STAND AT THE DINING ROOM WINDOW, DRINKING A CUP OF tea. I watch the bees dance amongst the sunflowers. The butterflies float above the roses. For weeks, there has been a monarch here, and when I see it flash in the sunlight, I always think of my mother. Partly because of the monarch tattoo she'd had on her hip, but also because butterflies are supposed to be the dead waving a little hello to the ones they've left behind.

Today there are two monarchs. They glide past the window, past the roses, and out over the yard. They twirl around each other, a playful game of tag that soars high then dips low.

They seem happy to be together.

I watch them until they flutter out of sight, disappearing beneath the branches of my neighbor's weeping cherry tree.

They've gone on. They have other things to do. Places to be.

That leaves me. And this tricky business of living.

Me. With a lifetime laid before me.

Opportunities to embrace peace, to find happiness and joy after so much sadness.

A chance to move forward, unburdened by my past.

It's a little scary, I admit, all of this possibility. The idea I don't need to rely on my fear anymore. Or all of this anxiety. I can hardly imagine what shape these tools might take in a new life.

But I want to try something else. I *have* to try.

If I ever start to doubt myself, start to believe that a liberated life is impossible after so much loss—in the moments where everything inside me wants to turn back to what I've always known—I'll just remember what my mother always told me:

Baby, you've got this.

AUTHOR'S NOTE

First and foremost, I want to thank everyone, from the bottom of my heart, who came this far into the story with me. It has meant so much that you've allowed me to share my mother's story with you as I tried to make sense of my loss and understand her death.

I've taken you as far as I can, since as of writing this, I don't know what will happen next. As I mentioned, I haven't heard back from the medical examiner or the detective. I have doubts that this will ever see a fair trial.

And while I absolutely believe, in my heart of hearts, that Joe is the one responsible for my mom's death, I can't help but ask, who killed my mother? Truly?

Was it the father that raped her when she was a child? The man who broke her spirit, her mind? Was it the mother who silenced her? Was it the pharmaceutical industry that does a poor job of regulating how and when doctors hand out pills, and what profits can be turned off of over-medicating others to the point of addiction? Was it the lack of a well-funded mental health system that left her largely untreated, unsupported?

Or might we even blame something as nebulous as capitalism, a structure hell-bent on keeping the poor *poor*. The sick *sick*, regardless of whose lives are destroyed in the process.

I have to say that as guilty as Joe is, I think they're all a bit to blame.

Regardless of whether Joe ever goes to prison for what he did or not, there are things that I hope will come of this story, and if you don't mind spending a little more time with me, I'd love to share my hopes with you.

Maybe if we both wish hard enough, they will come true.

1. I HOPE THIS STORY HELPS SOMEONE.

My mother struggled with many things in her life. Childhood abuse, alcoholism, addiction, domestic violence, and mental illness. If any of these things touch your life, I hope that hearing her story made you feel less alone.

Maybe you or someone you love has a history of abuse, or maybe you're still in the thick of it. Or perhaps you're like me, and you're in the difficult position of watching your loved one suffer, and feeling absolutely helpless to stop it.

Whatever the situation, I hope this story made you realize that you deserve better. I want you to know that. It doesn't matter what happened to you. It doesn't matter what you've done or haven't done in order to survive another day. It doesn't matter if you have a mental illness or an addiction—you deserve to be happy. To experience joy and love—I want this and many other good things for you. I'm sure *a lot* of people want that for you, whether or not you're in a place to realize it.

Please know that what's happening or has happened to

you isn't personal. You're not being punished. You aren't a bad person. All of this is simply the result of a bad situation, made worse by a broken system that doesn't offer enough support to people who need it.

2. IF YOU'VE SUFFERED A LOSS, I HOPE THIS STORY GIVES YOU PERMISSION TO GRIEVE.

I probably don't tell you that in many places—America in particular—it's almost like we don't have permission to grieve. Maybe it's our jobs, which expect us to show up on Monday come hell, highwater, or murdered mothers.

Maybe it's our own friends and families who are uncomfortable with our feelings and wish we would just buck up. Whatever the reason, we aren't allowed to fall apart. If we can't sleep, eat, shower, or continue on with our responsibilities, it's seen as a personal failing rather than the by-product of grief.

I'm also surprised again and again by how many people don't realize they're grieving—myself included. This can be either because we were told at an early age to disregard any inconvenient emotions or because, again, we simply aren't taught what grief is or what to do with it.

But *any* loss can cause grief, not just when someone dies. The loss of a relationship, a friendship, a job, or opportunity. An illness can instigate a loss of the way we used to live, how we can use our bodies. Not to mention that many of us are grieving now with the losses incurred by the pandemic. This grief may be felt for a while, so I encourage you to do a bit of research for yourself and see if you have the symptoms, because recognizing your own grief is the first step.

If you are grieving, this is me giving you permission to fall apart. No matter what the world or maybe even the people around you tell you, you deserve this time, this space. Take it.

Go slow. Be gentle. It doesn't mean you're weak or pathetic. It means you cared about someone or something. It means your heart is still working. Believe me, this is cause to celebrate.

I also hope that if you *can* find someone in your life to share your grief with, a good friend or your family, or maybe even professionals, that you *do* share your grief. It can be really, really hard to let other people see us in pain, but it's so much easier than trying to carry on alone.

That was why it was so challenging for me to tell this story. Even though it's true that my fiction often showcases characters who've lost someone they love, it was easier to present this grief when I could pretend that it wasn't my own. It's very different when we fall apart in front of someone and we're afraid of what they might think of us.

So my second wish is that if you have grief work to do, I hope that you find the time, space, support, and courage to do it.

3. I HOPE THIS STORY GIVES YOU PERMISSION TO TAKE CARE OF YOURSELF.

Whether it's saving yourself from a more immediate danger like domestic violence or substance abuse, or if you need to rebuild your relationship with yourself and address your own traumas—whatever it is, I hope this story emphasizes how important it is to take care of yourself.

That you're worth taking care of.

The single most helpful aspect of my own healing has been self-care. Self-care is a practice so often overlooked or rejected in Western cultures. We take pride in the fact that we are busy, overworked, stressed to our cores. Or worse, we make self-care glossy, shiny, and inaccessible, saying it's a bubble bath with rose petals or another bottle of wine. Then we wonder why it doesn't really work.

Building a relationship with myself saved me. When I came out of my childhood I was so disconnected from my emotional and physical needs that I basically had to learn everything from scratch.

I hope you're in a better place than that, but if you aren't, if in fact you have a long way to go, don't be discouraged. You'll be so glad that you gave yourself this amazing gift.

If self-care still sounds like some weird woo-woo idea and you never know what it means when people bring it up, let me offer this definition.

Self-care is having a good relationship with yourself. And in this good relationship are the practices and habits you do that restore your sense of well-being. I've also heard it described as a "sequence of pleasant events." Effective self-care tasks vary from person to person, so it will take some time for you to figure out what makes you feel loved and cared for. There's a great list that you might like in *Own Your Greatness*, a book by Dr. Lisa Orbé-Austin and Dr. Richard Orbé-Austin.

But here are some things that help me: spending time in nature, cloud gazing, stargazing, getting fresh air, or bird watching. Hiking or walking. Going to the beach. Journaling. Reading. Exercising. Not eating too much sugar. Mindfulness. Eating in nice restaurants. Getting some kind of body care like a massage, or my hair or nails done, or a facial. Painting. Receiving flowers, even if I buy them for myself. Listening to music, practicing gratitude, dancing like a fool. Browsing a bookstore. Freestyling on my piano. Talking to a good friend. Or baking myself something delicious. Snuggling my dog. Singing normal songs and sentences as opera: "Hon-NEE! Should I take out the *TRASH*?"

Whatever it is that gives you joy, I hope you do it. I really can't oversell you on this idea that you should use your life to do the things that bring you joy.

4. I HOPE THIS STORY WILL PROTECT A CHILD.

My mother's mental illness and addiction problems stemmed from her chronic sexual and psychological abuse. I hope that by listening to her story, someone will recognize the symptoms of abuse and step in to protect a child from being abused.

We can't underestimate the prevalence of childhood abuse. Fifty-one percent of girls and 48.6% of boys will experience childhood abuse. Seventy-six percent of childhood abuse experiences are perpetrated by their parents. In the case of sexual abuse, the CDC says one in four girls and one in thirteen boys will experience sexual abuse, and that 91% of the time, the abuse will happen by someone they know.[1]

We *have* to keep our eyes open. We have to notice when a child's behavior changes. If they suddenly dislike an activity or environment, or don't want to spend time with a person. If they become depressed, socially withdrawn, or they start doing poorly in school. They might even develop hysterical seizures like my mother did. Whatever the changes may be, we have to pay attention, and **if we see something, we have to say something.**

5. I HOPE THIS STORY INSPIRES CHANGE, PARTICULARLY IN THE MENTAL HEALTH SYSTEM AND JUSTICE SYSTEM.

America—and I'm sure other parts of the world—needs an overhaul in its mental healthcare and justice systems.

It isn't enough to just step in and save a child once the damage has already begun. More can be done to head off the causes of child abuse before they happen. Now that we know that four or more adverse childhood experiences increases a person's risk of physical and mental health illnesses, we should do what we can to prevent those adverse experiences from occurring.

We can do this by strengthening economic support for families, promoting social norms that protect against violence, and ensuring a strong start for children through early childhood home visitations, high-quality childcare, and preschool enrichment programs. We can invest in skills, teach social-emotional learning, safe dating and healthy relationship dynamics, parenting skills, invest in mentoring and after-school programs. Offer more victim-centered services, enhanced primary care, family-centered treatment for substance abuse, and more.

As for the justice system, I don't need to point out how *very* unjust it is that a black man can go to prison for life for a crime he didn't do, while someone like my uncle can have a hundred dropped charges, many of them violent, and escape any significant responsibility for his actions.

Part of this justice system reform should involve addressing rapists and abusers. I wish I could say that domestic and sexual violence like what my mother experienced was a rare occurrence, but we know it's not. The most dangerous risk to a woman's life is having a partner, and three women are murdered by their partners every day.[2] We need to teach men and boys not to rape, and we need to hold them accountable when they do rather than give them lenient sentences or put their needs, reputations, and well-being above the well-being of the women they've hurt. When we don't do this, when we fail to protect and vindicate the victims, they are left to struggle with their feelings of worthlessness the way my mother struggled, for the rest of their lives.

I hope that prisons will stop being for-profit machines that punish poverty, race, and unresolved trauma, enslaving millions, and become instead an avenue for something significantly more useful. Maybe together, with a functional and well-funded mental health care system, we can create something that actually works. A system that protects people. A system that heals people.

These are my hopes for the future and for you. These are the things I will continue to wish for in the coming days. It's true that I cannot change what happened to my mother. I cannot give her her life back or undo all the pain she endured.

But I also refuse to believe that her life was meaningless. That absolutely nothing can be done.

Because I'm still here. And so are you.

THANK YOU!

Did you enjoy this book? You can make a BIG difference.

I don't have the same power as big New York publishers who can buy full-spread ads in magazines, and you won't see my covers on the side of a bus anytime soon, but what I *do* have are wonderful readers like you.

And honest reviews from readers garner more attention for my books and help my career more than anything else I could possibly do—and I can't get a review without you! So if you would be so kind, I'd be very grateful if you would post a review for this book.

It only takes a minute or so of your time, and yet you can't imagine how much it helps me. It can be as short as you like, and whether positive or negative, it really does help. I appreciate it so much and so do the readers looking for their next favorite read.

If you would be so kind, please find your preferred retailer and leave a review for this book today.

With much gratitude,
Kory

GET YOUR FREEBIES TODAY

Thank you so much for reading *Who Killed My Mother?* I hope my mother's story helped or served you in some way. If you liked my storytelling, good news! There's a lot more of it out in the world. The best way to learn more about me and all that I do is to join my newsletter. It's free and you can unsubscribe at the click of a button anytime you want. Plus when you join, you get lots of freebies: my mother's autopsy report, family photographs, free ebooks and more.

So if you'd like to join, please sign up here ➜ www.whokilledmymother.com/newsletter

As to the newsletter itself, I send out 2-3 emails per month and host a monthly giveaway exclusively for my subscribers. The prizes are usually signed books or other goodies I think you'll enjoy. I also share information about my current projects and personal anecdotes (like pictures of my dog).

I do love connecting with readers this way, so I hope you'll join us. If emails aren't your thing—no matter how fun they are—you can always visit www.whokilledmymother.com or www.korymshrum.com to say hello instead, or follow me on social media.

Either way, thank you again for reading and I hope to hear from you soon.

ACKNOWLEDGMENTS

It is an understatement to say that I never expected to write a book like this. I intended spend the rest of my days writing and selling my dark fiction, pawning it off as a product of an imaginative mind. When I needed a break from that, there was the anxiety poetry.

What a life.

Yet here we are, and the book is done, but it would not have been possible without a great deal of support. Hats off to my good friend Jasie Gale for her help with the cover and cleaning up the family photographs—which really were in bad shape. Many thanks to Toby Selwyn my editor who agreed to do this project even though he much prefers meeting Lou Thorne in dark alleys for a good gun fight. We also can't forget Alexandra Amor, my wonderful assistant, who helped in so many ways that it would be hard to mention each task here. Everything from book production, formatting, interior styling, to web design and so on—all those magical assistant things she does.

So I'll simply say: thank you for all of it, A.

Then of course there are the friends and beloveds who

talked me through what was probably one of the most difficult years I'd had in a very long time. It was very twisty, wasn't it? In the dictionary beside *emotional rollercoaster*, there's my face, circa 2020.

Yet everyone I needed was there: Kimberly Benedicto, Kathrine Pendleton, Angela Roquet, Monica La Porta, Victoria Solomon, Adison Purchase. Matthew and Elizabeth who sent flowers when my mom died. Uncle Craig and Aunt Alex who listened to me talk about my mom. Mariah Taylor for proofing every single episode of the podcast before I published it. Let's not forget Charley, pug companion extraordinaire, who would let me hug him, squish him and cry into his fur without asking any questions.

Then there were the countless others who, through every kind word and loyal moment, reminded me just how very far I've come in the last fifteen years.

Fifteen years.

That's how long it's been since 23-year-old Kory began taking her first terrified steps toward a better life. If she hadn't been brave enough to dream it, to want it, I wouldn't have anything.

She's really the one I have to thank for all of this. I will forever be grateful for her hard work, blood, sweat, tears, and heartfelt determination.

She did the work. She didn't believe she could, but she gave it her all anyway against all the odds.

And look at us now.

Thanks for everything, kid.

ABOUT THE AUTHOR

Kory M. Shrum is author of the bestselling *Shadows in the Water* and *Dying for a Living* series, as well as several other novels. She has loved books and words all her life. She reads almost every genre you can think of, but when she writes, she writes science fiction, fantasy, and thrillers, or often something that's all of the above. She also publishes poetry under the name K.B. Marie.

In 2020, she launched a true crime podcast "Who Killed My Mother?", sharing the true story of her mother's tragic death. You can listen for free on YouTube or your favorite podcast app.

When not writing, eating, reading, or indulging in her true calling as a stay-at-home dog mom, she can usually be found under thick blankets with snacks. The kettle is almost always on.

She lives in Michigan with her equally bookish wife, Kim, and their rescue pug, Charley. Learn more at www.korymshrum.com

ALSO BY KORY M. SHRUM

FICTION

Dying for a Living series

Dying for a Living

Dying by the Hour

Dying for Her: A Companion Novel

Dying Light

Worth Dying For

Dying Breath

Dying Day

Shadows in the Water: Lou Thorne Thrillers

Shadows in the Water

Under the Bones

Danse Macabre

Carnival

Devil's Luck

What Comes Around

Castle Cove series

Welcome to Castle Cove

Night Tide

The City / 2603 novels

The City Below

The City Within

The City Outside

POETRY (AS K.B. MARIE)

Birds and Other Dreamers

Questions for the Dead

You Can't Keep It

Then Came Love

NON-FICTION

Who Killed My Mother? a memoir

You can also support her on Patreon or visit her website to learn more about her work.

BIBLIOGRAPHY

Brown, Brené. *The Power of Vulnerability: Teachings of Authenticity, Connection, and Courage.* Louisville, CO: Sounds True, 2013

Orbé-Austin, Dr. Lisa and Orbé-Austin, Dr. Richard. *Own Your Greatness: Overcome Impostor Syndrome, Beat Self-Doubt, and Succeed in Life.* Brooklyn, NY: Ulysses Press, 2020

van der Kolk, Bessel. *The Body Keeps the Score: Brain, Mind, and Body in the Healing of Trauma.* New York: Penguin Books, 2014

Wolynn, Mark. *It Didn't Start With You: How Inherited Family Trauma Shapes Who We Are and How to End the Cycle.* New York: Penguin Life, 2016

NOTES

CHAPTER 5

1. Nancy Glass, PhD, MPH, RN, Associate Professor. Non-fatal strangulation is an important risk factor for homicide of women. https://www.ncbi.nlm.nih.gov/pmc/articles/PMC2573025/

CHAPTER 11

1. Jean Goodwin, Mary Simms, and Robert Bergman. Hysterical seizures: a sequel to incest. https://pubmed.ncbi.nlm.nih.gov/495709/

CHAPTER 12

1. Centers for Disease Control and Prevention. https://www.cdc.gov/violenceprevention/aces/index.html
2. Mayo Clinic. Antisocial personality disorder. https://www.mayoclinic.org/diseases-conditions/antisocial-personality-disorder/symptoms-causes/syc-20353928

CHAPTER 13

1. Centers for Disease Control and Prevention. Preventing child sexual abuse. https://www.cdc.gov/violenceprevention/childabuseandneglect/childsexualabuse.html
2. US National Library of Medicine. Domestic violence in the 1970s. https://circulatingnow.nlm.nih.gov/2015/10/15/domestic-violence-in-the-1970s/
3. US Department of Labor. Office of the Assistant Secretary for Administration and Management. Equal pay for equal work. https://www.dol.gov/agencies/oasam/centers-offices/civil-rights-center/internal/policies/equal-pay-for-equal-work
4. US National Library of Medicine. Domestic violence in the 1970s. https://circulatingnow.nlm.nih.gov/2015/10/15/domestic-violence-in-the-1970s/

5. Steven F. Maier and Martin E. P. Seligman. Learned Helplessness at Fifty: Insights from Neuroscience. https://www.ncbi.nlm.nih.gov/pmc/articles/PMC4920136/

CHAPTER 17

1. National Institute on Drug Abuse. What is fentanyl? https://www.drugabuse.gov/publications/drugfacts/fentanyl
2. American Addiction Centers. Fentanyl vs. Heroin: An Opioid Comparison Edited by Marisa Crane, B.S. https://americanaddictioncenters.org/fentanyl-treatment/similarities

CHAPTER 18

1. Drugs.com Fentanyl Overdose & Abuse. Medically reviewed by Leigh Ann Anderson, PharmD. https://www.drugs.com/illicit/fentanyl.html

AUTHOR'S NOTE

1. Centers for Disease Control and Prevention. Preventing child sexual abuse. https://www.cdc.gov/violenceprevention/childsexualabuse/fastfact.html
2. National Network to End Domestic Violence. Each day three women die because of of domestic violence. https://nnedv.org/content/each-day-three-women-die-because-of-domestic-violence/

Made in the USA
Columbia, SC
31 July 2022